LIBERATING

FAITH

REIMAGINING CHRISTIAN EDUCATION AS TRANSFORMATIVE

JAMES I. CLARK

Seymour Press
Lanham MD

Liberating Faith: *Reimagining Christian Education as Transformative*

ISBN: 978-1-967034-29-1

Table of Contents

Acknowledgment

This work is the result of invaluable fellowship and dialogue with colleagues who serve the Body of Christ as educators, clergy, and authors. Their collective expertise and encouragement ultimately persuaded me to share these perspectives with a wider audience. I owe a profound debt of gratitude to Bishop Maurice D. Carter, my Chief of Staff and Executive Director of Region IV; Bishop Ernie L. Jackson, Pastor Emeritus of Grace Tabernacle in San Francisco, California; and Dr. Pamela Venable of The Crystal Cathedral in the Virginia Western Diocese of COOLJC. Finally, I am deeply grateful to Dr. Estrelda Alexander, President of Seymour Press, whose editorial mastery and immense patience guided this project to completion.

Foreword

Dr. James I. Clark, a revered leader, teacher, and former presider of the Church of Our Lord Jesus Christ of the Apostolic Faith, has devoted his life not only to proclaiming the gospel but also to educating the people of God. While many are lifelong learners, Clark has distinguished himself as a lifelong educator— driven by a deep quest for knowledge and a profound commitment to sharing that knowledge for the strengthening and maturation of the church. His academic journey, which culminated in two doctoral degrees in education, began with a sacred calling to form minds, as well as hearts, for faithful service to Christ.

This work emerges from decades of pastoral leadership, theological reflection, and educational advocacy within the African American Apostolic Pentecostal tradition. Clark writes as one who has stood at the intersection of spiritual fervor and intellectual responsibility, convinced that the vitality of Pentecostal faith must be sustained by thoughtful engagement with Scripture, history, and culture. For him, Christian education is not a departure from the Spirit's work, but a means by which the Spirit guides the Church into truth.

Rooted in the legacy of the Azusa Street Revival and the formation of Apostolic Pentecostal identity, this book traces Pentecostal theological development while calling it toward renewed purpose. Clark challenges us to move beyond inherited assumptions and interpretive schemes that obscure the original Scriptural intent, examining presuppositions and eisegesis that have, at times, stunted understanding. In doing so, he proposes that Christian education can be a means of liberation — guiding believers toward deeper engagement with the historical, grammatical, and spiritual context of the biblical text so that faith might be both fervent and informed.

Clark insists that holiness cannot be confined to personal piety, but must express itself in compassionate action on behalf of the marginalized and oppressed. His work calls the church to remember that the power of the Holy Spirit is given not only for worship, but also for witness in the world. At the heart of this vision lies the prophetic call of Micah 6:8 to do justice, love mercy, and walk humbly with God—a summons to a faith that is both deeply spiritual and courageously engaged.

This work represents more than a historical survey or theological argument; it is a summons to maturation. In it, Clark invites Pentecostal Christians to grow beyond inherited patterns of thought toward a faith that is intellectually responsible, spiritually vibrant, and socially responsive. He envisions a community of believers who love the church deeply enough to challenge it and who remain rooted in Apostolic heritage while embracing the intellectual formation necessary to address the complexities of contemporary life with wisdom and grace.

His life bears witness to the truth that genuine leadership requires both fidelity to tradition as well as the courage to pursue growth. It reminds us that education, when guided by the Holy Spirit, is not an enemy of faith, but a means of grace.

As one who has witnessed the unfolding of Pentecostal history across decades of ministry, I commend this work to pastors, educators, students, and all believers who desire a deeper understanding of Pentecostal heritage and a clearer vision for the future of the movement. May it inspire renewed commitment to pursue truth, practice justice, and humbly walk in faith that honors God and blesses humanity.

Bishop Dr. Ernest L. Jackson
Pastor Emeritus,
San Francisco, California

Preface

This book begins from the premise that Christian education is most faithfully understood as a formative, constructive practice rather than a primarily transmissive one. *Liberating Faith: Reimagining Christian Education as Transformation* examines how pedagogical assumptions, curricular choices, and institutional habits shape theological imagination and moral agency in Christian congregational and educational settings. Drawing on dialogue with educators, students, and ministry leaders, this work argues for approaches to teaching and learning that integrate critical reflection, communal discernment, and spiritual formation.

Across the chapters, I propose a liberative account of Christian education that is attentive to both theological tradition and contemporary challenges. The analysis attends to the ways educational practices can perpetuate constraint—through unexamined power, exclusionary norms, or impoverished conceptions of knowledge—and considers pedagogical alternatives oriented toward justice, intellectual rigor, and ecclesial responsibility. The goal is to offer a framework and set of guiding principles that practitioners and scholars can adapt to diverse contexts, from classrooms and catechetical programs to congregational formation and leadership development.

The intended audience includes Christian education teachers, clergy, lay leaders, parents, and students who are seeking conceptual clarity and practical direction for transformative formation. Readers may engage the book as a critical resource for evaluating existing educational models, as a constructive guide for curricular and pedagogical redesign, or as a prompt for sustained congregational conversation. If the book succeeds, it will contribute to renewed practices of teaching and learning that deepen discipleship while fostering reflective, responsible engagement with the social and cultural realities within which faith is lived.

Respectfully,
Apostle James I. Clark, Jr., MBA, M. Div., Ed.D.
April 2026

Chapter I

Introduction

The African American Apostolic Church was birthed within the young Pentecostal movement in 1916, when the "new issue" concerning the appropriate baptism formula for believers burst on the scene with disruptive force. The doctrinal issue regarding the Trinitarian formula recorded in Matthew 2:19 or in the name of Jesus Christ, according to Acts 2:38, was the first schism the newly formed Pentecostal movement had to face, and dissent over the matter split the movement.

Those holding to the Acts 2:38 formula questioned belief in the idea of the Trinity, that the one God eternally exists as three distinct 'persons': the Father, the Son (Jesus Christ), and the Holy Spirit. Others argued for a radical unity in the Godhead consistent with the Hebrew Scripture's teaching of the Oneness of God. They insisted that all who had been baptized according to the Matthew passage be rebaptized.

The hostilities that surfaced within the recently formed body demonstrate the depth of the fission, as many relationships were broken while new ones were established. Things came to a head at a fall 1916 meeting of its General Council, forcing a split in an organization that came into being only two years earlier. To stave off changes in their baptismal practice, leaders adopted a seventeen-point "Statement of Fundamental Truths". "But out of the 585 ministers who composed the council, 156 refused to accept it.

After the split, the Oneness group reorganized as the General Assembly of Apostolic Assemblies. Garfield Thomas (G. T.) Haywood of the Pentecostal Assemblies of the World worked with the ministers of this short-lived organization to arrange a merger between the two groups. Haywood had held credentials since 1911, so association with him helped ministers obtain credentials that exempted them from military service and gave them access to other benefits. The group sought to transcend racial differences, but also soon experienced a split along racial lines. As executive secretary, Haywood had tremendous appeal with African American ministers, but their increased numbers caused a split in the organizations. Today, all these churches are, in some way, connected with either the Pentecostal Assemblies of the World or an early denomination that came out of it.

This book begins with examining the background from which Pentecostal churches emerged. Then it provides an overview of two major Apostolic denominations: the parent body, PAW, and the largest Oneness body, the Church of Our Lord Jesus Christ (COOLJC), that emerged from the earlier body.

Although the Azusa Street Revival link the movement with Wesleyan and Holiness groups, their primary theological framework is dispensational premillennialism.

This understanding constrains its willingness to take agency for transforming the world. From the turn of the twentieth century, this worldview has heavily influenced the doctrine of African American Pentecostals and Apostolics, as well as other Fundamentalists and Evangelicals.

Thus, most Pentecostals and Apostolics view their mission as precluding involvement in efforts for social change. This worldview limits the church's role in salvation history to that of an otherworldly bystander. Yet, Jesus challenged his disciples to go into the world and be "salt" and "light" in a way that "men might see their good works and glorify (God) which is in heaven."[1]

Though the movement has been cautious about engaging with black and womanist theologies, fearing contamination by secular ideologies, the insights of both can contribute to an understanding of the context in which the contemporary African American Apostolic church operates. This work attempts to do just that. It is essential to provide effective strategies for acting in accordance with the Lord's command within today's world. Ultimately, our theology must be refined through rigorous evaluation and integration of previously neglected resources for Christian education, in a manner that fosters a faith community capable of acting as a transformative change agent.

---

[1] Matthew 5:13-16,

Chapter II

The Emergence of Pentecostalism

The Azusa Street Revival

Pentecostalism was spawned in the first decade of the twentieth century in the confluence of Wesleyan Perfectionism, the Keswick "higher life" movement, and the black Holiness movement. During a call for another Pentecost, many Holiness revivalists shifted their focus from entire sanctification to seeking the baptism with the Holy Spirit, driven by a desire for the empowerment for service, which was believed to come with this experience.

Interest grew in divine healing stemming from the atonement of Christ and as a consequence of entire sanctification.[1] A. B. Simpson, "four-square doctrine" of salvation, baptism with the Holy Spirit, divine healing, and the Second Coming of Christ.[2] Leaders on "the Reformed side of the Holiness movement,"[3] such as Reuben A. Torrey, A. J. Gordon, Dwight L. Moody, Arthur Pierson, and A. B. Simpson emerged as the principal architects of this theology[4] and the Pentecostal impulse, with its four

---

[1] Dayton, *The Theological Roots of Pentecostalism*. Waco, TX: Baker Academic, 1987, 126-129.

[2] Ibid.

[3] Peter Prosser, *Eschatology and Its Influence on American and British Religious Movements*. Lewiston, ME: Edwin Mellen Press, 1999, 19.

[4] Ibid., 18-19.

theological themes,[5] to become widely accepted among the more radical revivalists.

The understandings of sanctification, empowerment, and premillennialism were sustained by a web of national, regional, and local associations, conferences, summer camps, publications, and Bible colleges and institutes. The practice of faith healing was undergirded by a chain of faith homes that stretched across the Northeast and Midwest in the latter quarter of the century. Charles Cullis began his Faith Cure House in Boston in 1864 by opening a home for incurable tuberculosis patients. Cullis expanded his efforts to include multiple homes catering to those with cancer, spinal diseases, orphans, and the destitute. The ministry served thousands of patients, with many reportedly coming to Christian faith. A. B. Simpson began Berachah House in his private residence but soon relocated and expanded it to accommodate an increasing number of guests impacted by Simpson's ministry. As early as the late 1880s and 1890s, Dowie and other evangelists, such as Woodworth-Etter, crisscrossed the country with their outdoor tent campaigns and spectacular healing rallies.[6] By 1900, his Zion City was a communitarian theocracy devoted to personal asceticism and faith healing.

These homes, and the traveling revivals led by Dowie and Woodworth-Etter, and others, played a crucial role in spreading the message of healing and spiritual empowerment, laying the groundwork for the Pentecostal

---

[5] Ibid., 28.
[6] Ibid., 20.

emphasis on supernatural manifestations. The interconnectedness of these ministries and their widespread appeal helped prepare the soil for the emergence of Pentecostalism, as individuals drawn by the promise of divine healing, personal sanctification, and anticipation of Christ's imminent return became receptive to the distinctive doctrines and practices that would soon define the movement.

Out of this vortex, Charles Fox Parham unified the four prominent theological themes of the revivalist factions into his Apostolic faith theology and focused on finding biblical evidence of the baptism of the Holy Spirit.[7] He instructed his Topeka Bible school students to study Acts 2 and "fast and pray for a revival of Pentecostal power."[8]

Out of this search, on January 1, 1900, Agnes Ozman, one of his students, received the experience of speaking in tongues. Thereafter, Parham and all the students received the experience.[9] He named this expression the "biblical evidence" of baptism of the Holy Spirit.[10] Parham coupled this understanding with J. Nelson Darby's teaching of the soon-coming end of the world,[11] and began to preach that a

---

[7] Ibid., 6-14. Methodist and Holiness preacher, Charles Parham, founded a Bible school in Topeka, Kansas in 1900. He was convinced that the end of the world was coming, but that God would give the world one last chance to repent by sending a revival of faith in Jesus Christ. Thus, he asked his students to fast and pray for a revival of 'Pentecostal power' such as on the day of Pentecost.

[8] Ibid., 7-8.

[9] Ibid.

[10] Ibid., 6.

[11] Ibid. John N. Darby was the leader of the Plymouth Brethren who introduced dispensational eschatology with such themes as the 'Rapture," etc.

special Holy Spirit baptism was available to believers to prepare them for the Second Coming of Christ."[12]

After carrying his message across the Southwest, Parham settled in Houston, Texas, in 1905, where he set up another Bible school. Here, black Holiness preacher Lucy Farrow, who was already pastoring a small Holiness mission, came into contact with him when Parham conducted a revival campaign. During this campaign, Farrow began working with his team as a cook while continuing as a Holiness worker.

She introduced him to William J. Seymour, another Black holiness preacher, who had encountered the movement through Daniel Sidney (D.S.) Warner's Evening Light Saints. This group sought a restoration of the New Testament Church's purity and unity and believed God was bringing renewed spiritual illumination in the "evening" of time. They also emphasized entire sanctification, unity among believers, divine healing, and holy living, but rejected denominational structures.[13]

Parham's introduction of the subject of initial evidence of speaking in tongues[14] arrested Seymour's attention and inspired him to attend the Bible school.[15] When the racial

---

[12] Ibid.

[13] James S. Tinney, "William J. Seymour: Father of Modern-Day Pentecostalism, *Journal of the Interdenominational Theological Center*. 4:1 (Fall 1978), 13. Like many of the Holiness groups, The Evening Light Saints taught that the second experience of entire sanctification freed the Christian from all sinfulness of the heart and the inner man." When Seymour heard their testimonies, he went to the altar and "prayed through" to sanctification and became a preacher within the movement.

[14] Ibid

[15] Ibid., 14. Seymour received information about the doctrine Lucy Farrow, who told him of seemingly strange wonder, including the possibility of a third religious

barriers of the South would not allow him to join the white students in the classroom, he sat outside an open door to hear the lectures.[16] Under the banner of Parham's Apostolic movement, both men ran successful revival meetings in the city,[17] with Seymour working primarily within the Black community, while he attended Farrow's Holiness mission.

There he met and befriended Neely Terry, another black saint, Los Angeles resident who was visiting family in Houston. After hearing Seymour preach, she returned home with such a favorable impression that she convinced her pastor, Julia Hutchins, to invite him to assist with her mission church. Seymour answered the call.[18]

In his first message to Hutchins' congregation, Seymour attempted to correct the misunderstanding about the baptism of the Holy Spirit."[19] For he told the congregants that they had not received the Holy Ghost, since they had not spoken in tongues, but were only sanctified. The leadership rejected Seymour's teaching, and Hutchins barred him from the church.[20] So when he returned for the afternoon service, he found the door padlocked.

---

experience which would give him added spiritual power and enable him to speak in languages he had not learned. Although Seymour had problems with the speaking in tongues before hearing her story, he desired more spiritual power, so he decided to look into this new phenomenon

[16] H. Vinson Synan, "Seymour, William Joseph (1870-1922)," in Dictionary of Pentecostal and Charismatic Movements. Stanley M. Burgess et. al., eds. (Grand Rapids, MI: Zondervan Publishing House, 1988, 780-81. Parham was a segregationist and did not allow Seymour to sit in the classroom with the white students. Nevertheless, Seymour accepted what he learned from the hallway. He embraced the teaching, though he had not experienced glossolalia at the time.

[17] Prosser, *Dispensationalist Eschatology,* 11.

[18] Tinney, "In the Tradition of William Seymour," 15.

[19] Ibid.

[20] Ibid.

A sympathetic couple, Edward and Mattie Lee, took Seymour into their home and provided a place for his lodging. Ruth and Richard Asberry allowed him to hold prayer meetings at their home.

"Seymour's response to the 'bolted door' was to hold cottage meetings, which the Lord miraculously transformed into an 'international gateway for the Pentecostal movement."[21] So many people responded to his message that large groups would assemble to pray and tarry for the baptism of the Holy Ghost.[22]

But though he received a favorable response to his teaching, after a few weeks, no one had received evidence of speaking in tongues. So, he reached out to Farrow and his close friend Joseph Warren, another evangelist who was working with Parham, to join him in Los Angeles to help with this new mission. This invitation proved to be the catalyst that was needed.[23]

Within a few days of her arrival, the revival broke out in earnest, and one person after another began receiving the experience of tongues. One early recipient was brother Lee. While eating dinner in his home on April 9, 1906, Farrow rose from her seat, walked over to him, and said, "The Lord tells me to lay hands on you for the Holy Ghost." When she did, he fell out of his chair as though dead, and began speaking in tongues.[24] Then they went over to the prayer

---

[21] Lovett, "Black Origins of the Pentecostal Movement" in Synan, ed., *Aspects of Pentecostal,* 138.

[22] Ibid.

[23] Ibid.

[24] Ibid.

meeting at the Asberry's home. Six people were already on their knees, praying when, as he walked through the door, he lifted his hands and began to speak in tongues. The power fell on the others, and all six began to speak in tongues.[25]

By April 12, Seymour and several others had received the experience of tongues speech.

People from around the world visited the Azusa mission and shared in the outpouring.[26] People of different races and both genders participated equally in this extraordinary event, for Seymour had envisioned "a truly color-blind congregation."[27] While the interracialism was short-lived, the revival intensified over the next few years, with the most dramatic period believed to have been from 1906 through 1908.[28]

After that time, Pentecostal groups proliferated throughout the South and West, and several missions opened in the Los Angeles area. Some formed because

---

[25] Ibid., 16. [See also "How Pentecost Came to Los Angeles: An Eyewitness Account of the Momentous Events of the Year 1906." *Pentecostal Evangel* (April 8, 1956): 5.

[26] James I. Clark. Jr., "The Relationship of Theology and Social Action in The Black Apostolic Tradition." (M. Div. Thesis: Union Theological Seminary, 1990) Seymour heralded the outpouring, saying, "God makes no difference in nationality. Ethiopians, Chinese, Indians, Mexicans, and other nationalities worship together. The people are melted together; 100 made one lump, one bread, all one body in Christ Jesus." "The Spirit of the Apostolic Faith." *The Apostolic Faith* 1:6,(February – March 1907).

[27] Synan, Aspects of Pentecostal. 970 and Cecil M Robeck, Jr., "Azusa Street Revival," in *Dictionary of Pentecostal and Charismatic Movements*, Stanley M. Burgess et. al. eds. Grand Rapids, MI: Zondervan Publishing House, 1988), 36. (See Iain MacRoberts, *Black Roots and White Racism in Early Pentecostalism*. (New York: St. Martin's Press, 1988, 82. According to him, the interracial phenomenon occurred in America's most racist period, those from 1890-1920.... among the groups that had traditionally been most at odds: poor whites and poor black

[28] Synan, *Dictionary*, 780.

whites were unwilling to remain under the leadership of a black man. Others, like Frank Bartleman, were afraid that, like its Holiness predecessors, the movement would become cold and formal to become more acceptable to the Mainline Churches.[29]

The "Finished Work Controversy" between Seymour and popular preacher William Durham caused a major rift. The famed Chicago pastor opposed the Holiness doctrine most Pentecostals held of sanctification occurring after salvation as a "second step" or a "second work of grace." He argued, instead, that rather than a distinct, single moment, subsequent to salvation Christ's work on Calvary is received by believers at justification, with sanctification unfolding over the entire Christian's life.[30]

Though disagreements continued, Pentecostal teaching continued to spread across the nation, as well as to many other countries. Many who experienced the baptism of the Holy Spirit sought to fulfill the Lord's command to the disciples to be "… witnesses… unto the utmost parts of the earth."[31]

---

[29]This was not unique to whites, as David Daniels points out that tensions developed over C.P. Jones' and C.H. Mason's unwillingness to continue under the restrictions imposed by Baptist organizations. "The Cultural Renewal of Slave Religion: Charles Price Jones and the Emergence of the Holiness Movement in Mississippi, Ph.D. Dissertation, Union Theological Seminary, 1992. See also J. Laverne Tyson's, *Before I Sleep: A Narrative and Photographic Biography of Bishop Garfield Thomas Haywood*, Weldon Spring, MO: Pentecostal Publishing House, 1976, 149. According to him, many Pentecostals considered organizations unscriptural and anathema. They thought it would dilute the spontaneity of the Spirit.

[30] Synan, *Dictionary,* 780-81.

[31] Acts 1:8

Some believed they had been given a gift of languages for missionary work, went abroad. Lucy Leatherman made a trip around the world, while Frank Bartleman circled the globe once and made a second two-year evangelistic tour to Europe. Thomas Junk, as well as Bernt and Magna Bernsten, went to China. Martin L. Ryan led several young people to missions in the Philippines, Japan, and Hong Kong. George and Mary Berg and Alfred and Lillian Garr went to India, while Thomas Hezmalhalch and John G. Lake went to South Africa. Ansel H. Post became a long-term missionary to Egypt, and a host of mostly Black people, including Eduard and Mollie McGauley, George. W. and Daisy Batman, and Julia Hutchins took the Pentecostal message to Liberia.[32]

New Issue: Formation of Apostolic Pentecostalism

One of several new Apostolic Faith missions was the Pentecostal Assemblies of the World, which held its first meeting in Los Angeles in 1907.[33] An early minute book and ministerial record describe the event this way:

The general assembly of different "Pentecostal assemblies" that embraced the Pentecostal outpouring met in Los Angeles in October 1907. A Brother Pendleton was elected chairman pro tem, and a Brother Clark was elected secretary pro tem… The meeting focused on the introductory procedures for organizing all Pentecostal groups, including electing officers, establishing

---

[32] Robeck, *Dictionary*, 36.
[33] Ibid.

committees, crafting a constitution and bylaws, and establishing an official paper.[34]

For the next half a decade, these groups worked together more or less harmoniously. But a contentious idea that would further divide the movement emerged from an international revival held in 1913 at Arroyo Seco near Los Angeles. Prominent evangelist Mary Woodworth-Etter was the featured revivalist, and for most of the meeting, nothing out of the ordinary occurred.

Canadian evangelist Robert McAlister preached a baptismal sermon that contended that the proper formula for carrying out the ordinance was "in the name of Jesus." He insisted that this should replace the Trinitarian formula most Pentecostals were using at that time.

While many attendees heard this idea with some interest, it inspired, John G. Schepp to spend the night studying and praying about what he had heard. Early the next morning, Scheppe ran through the camp declaring that the Lord had shown him that this was true. This event is widely cited by historians as the "birth" of Oneness Pentecostalism. It led other prominent leaders, such as Frank J. Ewart and Glenn A. Cook, to begin preaching that baptism should be performed in the name of Jesus only and eventually to a rejection of the traditional doctrine of the Trinity. Not long after this, many believed the truth about baptism in Jesus' name.[35]

---

[34] The minute book of the Pentecostal Assemblies of the World, 1918 -1919, cited in Tyson, *Before I Sleep*, 188-89.

[35] Ibid.

Increasingly, many who had previously held and taught the Trinitarian baptismal formula accepted the new concept, and many of these would become members of the Assemblies of God, which was formed the next year. These advocates were insisting that anyone who had not been baptized in Jesus' name had to be re-baptized.[36] So, by the Spring of 1915, the new movement was spreading so rapidly that the aggressiveness of this new group and the speed with which their views were being accepted caused the Assemblies' leaders to challenge this doctrine.

But when Executive Presbyter, Eudorus N. Bell, one of its prominent leaders, was rebaptized, Assemblies of God members began to panic. Bell was editor of its two magazines, *Weekly Evangel* and *Word and Witness*.[37] In reaction to his capitulation, assistant editor J. Roswell Flower[38] took up the gauntlet against the "New Issue" and convinced the presbytery to call a meeting to stabilize the organization and "examine the issues."

Yet, the most they achieved was a strained, tentative truce.[39] The "New Issue" advocates pursued their course and not only continued to make inroads into the membership on the issue of baptism, but raised questions regarding the Trinitarian view of the Godhead.

---

[36] Reed.

[37] Ibid. Although Haywood was not a member of the Assembly of God, he had a strong fellowship with many of their churches. When he and 465 of his members were re-baptized, it shocked the Assemblies of God.

[38] Ibid. See references for Gary B. McGee, who writes that, "Flower Joseph James Roswell (1888-1970), Ann Alice Reynolds (1890)." 312.

[39] Ibid.

By the Fourth General Council in the Fall of 1916, Assemblies of God leaders presented Oneness advocates with a seventeen-point "Statement of Fundamental Truths" that included a strongly worded section affirming the traditional doctrine of the Trinity. The Oneness advocates refused to compromise, so when the vote was taken, 156 of 585 ministers and the many congregations that refused to accept the statement were ousted.[40]

Dissension over the two issues: rebaptism in Jesus' name and the validity of the doctrine of the Trinity, put the denomination on a collision course that led to the schism. Perhaps, had Oneness advocates not promoted their view so strongly as the only true course, acceptance of the Apostolic formula as an alternative baptismal formula would have settled the matter.[41]

The General Assembly of Apostolic Assemblies was formed in Eureka Springs, Arkansas, on December 28, 1916, by several leading ministers who left the Assemblies of God and emerged as leaders in a new organization.[42] With 154 ministers, missionaries, elders, deacons, and evangelists, the organization was short-lived since it lacked the authority to issue ministerial credentials, making its ministers eligible for the draft and ineligible for special clergy railroad rates.

In 1918, African American Oneness leader Garfield T. Haywood facilitated a merger between the General Assembly of Apostolic Assemblies and his small

---

[40] Ibid., 644.
[41] Ibid., 645.
[42] Reed, *Dictionary.* 645.

organization, the Pentecostal Assemblies of the World.[43] The merger was negotiated under the Pentecostal Assemblies of the World charter. With this move, Oneness Pentecostals seemed to have forged an integrated fellowship. At first, no racial distinction was made, and all racial barriers seemed to be wiped away. However, as believers moved out of the spiritual realm into the natural, race became a divisive issue.[44]

A schism occurred when PAW headquarters was moved to Haywood headquarters in Indianapolis, Indiana. As one of the three-member Board Directors, as well as General Secretary, Haywood's influence was formidable. The move to his hometown, his tremendous leadership and preaching ability, and his status as a leader changed the complexion of the Pentecostal Assemblies of the World from predominantly white to largely black.[45] The change resulted in black ministers leading most committees and holding most offices.[46] And this proved to be more than the white membership could handle, for they feared black domination.[47]

---

[43] Ibid., 645-646.

[44] Morris Golder, History oof the Pentecostal Assemblies of the World

[45] Ibid.

[46] Iain MacRoberts, *Black Roots and White Racism in Early Pentecostalism in the USA.* New York: St. Martin's Press, 1988), 72. He states that no blacks were present at the first meeting in 1918. At the second meeting in 1919, the office of Secretary passed from a white man, Booth Clibbon to G. T. Haywood who was black.

[47] Ibid. Reed describes Haywood as the most respected and popular of the black preachers, and with wide-ranging influence as a teacher, hymn writer, organizational leader, publisher, and an outspoken advocate for racial integration. See also, Morris E. Golder, *The Life and Works of Bishop Garfield Thomas Haywood 1880-1931).* Indianapolis, IN: Golder, 1977.

In November 1922, the southern white churches held a segregated "Southern Bible Conference." Soon after, they insisted that their fellowship cards be signed by the white leaders "… because of Jim Crow pressures in the South."[48] Yet, however, they were unable to explain to the Black ministers how anyone could determine the race of the signatories.

The 1924 Pentecostal Assemblies of the World Convention resulted in the final split, leading to two main Oneness groups: the Pentecostal Assemblies of the World and the Apostolic Assemblies General Association. Haywood led the PAW as Presiding Bishop until his death from a heart attack in 1931. [49]

At the time of his death, white ministers attempted to unify all the Oneness groups that had formed between 1924 and 1931, even offering a "racially balanced integrated structure," which several of the blacks eagerly embraced. But several black leaders objected to a swift merger as the Pentecostal Assemblies of Jesus Christ, fearing that insincere white negotiators were prompted by opportunism.[50]

The proposed compromise of changing the name and abandoning the Episcopal form of government practiced since 1925 was sufficient for ministers like Samuel Grimes, E. F. Akers, and AW. Lewis to take action.[51] They called for

---

[48] Ibid., 73. See also Morris E. Golder, *History of the Pentecostal Assemblies of the* World. Indianapolis, IN: Pentecostal Assemblies of the World, 1973, 43-45.

[49] Ibid., 75.

[50] Ibid.

[51] Ibid.

a reorganization meeting in Dayton, Ohio, where the predominantly black organization reemerged as an African-American Apostolic body under the Grimes' leadership.

Chapter III

Understanding the Church's Mission

The African American Apostolic World View

In his essay, "Black Religious Traditions: Sacred and Secular Themes," Gayraud Wilmore points out that the activities of Black independent churches were historically guided by a three-fold agenda: survival, liberation, and advancement of the Black race.[1] He charges that, with few exceptions, the contemporary Black church has failed to continue that tradition. Yet, miraculously, we have survived as a people, and the African-American Apostolic church has done little to work for social change for the race and other minorities.

And though African American leaders successfully resisted white attempts to dominate the Pentecostal Assemblies of the World, they embraced Fundamentalist doctrine that profoundly limited them. For the very thing they fought against ecclesiastically, they unwittingly allowed to happen intellectually when they bought into a premillennialist, dispensationalist, fundamentalist worldview that has hindered a more sanguine view of the church's role in advancing the liberation of oppressed communities. In embracing these views, African American

---

[1] Gayraud Wilmore, "Black Religious Traditions," in William R. Scott & William G. Shade, editors, *Upon These Shores: Themes in the African-American Experience, 1600 to the Present.* New York: Routledge, 2000, 285-298.

Apostolics abandoned their responsibility for social change that their forebearers inherited from involvement with other black churches.

Four themes: salvation, baptism in the Holy Spirit, divine healing, and the Second Coming of Christ comprise a "theological gestalt" that is the core of Pentecostal belief or the "logic of Pentecostalism."[2] They evolved from Wesleyan Methodism, through the Holiness revival movements, Oberlin Perfectionism, and the Keswick movement. Martin Marty asserts that pulling at any one of the four effects on the others as well as the whole. From the outset, they were dominant in Pentecostal teaching and the cornerstone of African-American Apostolic proclamation.

Since the first century, the Church has preached a Second Advent. For the next sixteen centuries, different degrees of emphasis and varying points of view colored this teaching. But it took on renewed prominence since the eighteenth century—especially in the latter part of the nineteenth and the first quarter of the twentieth century. Some scholars suggest this shift came about because of the increased emphasis on the work of the Holy Spirit in what is referred to as the "dispensation of the Spirit." Emil Brunner contends that we can trace in the history of Christendom something like a law, that the more vitally hope is present in the ecclesia… the more powerfully life in the Spirit of God is present…, the more urgent is its expectation of the coming of Jesus Christ; *so the fullness of*

---

[2] Dayton, *The Theological Roots*, 11.

the possession of the Spirit and the urgency of expectation are always found… as they were in the primitive community.[3]

While we may easily argue that the turn to a doctrine of the Holy Spirit in the late nineteenth century involved… a turn to eschatology, the rising impact of the nineteenth century premillennial movement became the model of Pentecostal education institutions.[4]

The history of premillennialism is complex. Its antecedents go beyond the nineteenth century or the Pentecostal movement to the sixteenth-century British millenarian movements and expectations that began to surface on the European Continent in reaction to the French Revolution.[5] This renewed emphasis on the apocalyptic sections of Scripture was a response to a major dilemma for which there were no easy answers and seemed to threaten the very existence of civilization.[6]

Marty refers to the phenomenon as an "alternative philosophy of history"[7] that opposes the modernist view and requires that those who embrace it "deal with the whole of history" and make a theological commitment. This approach expresses itself most dramatically when situations are so complex that the usual manner of interpreting them appears impossible.

---

[3] Emil Bruner, *Eternal Hope* Philadelphia: The Westminster Press, 1954, 59-60.

[4] Ibid., 145.

[5] Prosser, *Dispensationalist Eschatology,* 47.

[6] Ibid., 128.

[7] Martin E. Marty, *Modern American Religion.* Vol. 1. Chicago, IL: The University of Chicago Press, 1986, 218.

Donald Dayton examined Paul Hanson's explanation of shifts in thinking that brought about a different eschatological vision, replacing the postmillennial vision most evangelicals/revivalists embraced. This shift in vision signaled a transition from "prophetic eschatology" (the postmillennial vision) to "apocalyptic eschatology" (premillennial vision).

Prophetic eschatology seeks to make clear the divine will for God's kingdom and people, utilizing Old Testament examples to illustrate how the intentions of the divine council are realized within history. When circumstances *change so radically* that prophets can no longer provide clear guidance, *there is a shift* toward an apocalyptic eschatological perspective. In this mode, prophets cease interpreting the divine council in terms of tangible history, realpolitik, and human agency, often due to a prevailing pessimism rooted in adverse post-exilic conditions.

These explanations shed light on the cause of this radical shift from the postmillennial perspective that teaches that the world will be changed by the preaching of the Gospel first, and then the Second Advent will occur. The Church once felt positive about its role in affecting social change as part of its soul-saving mission. But after the last half of the nineteenth century, most Evangelical, Holiness, and Pentecostal movements began to hold a premillennial eschatology.

Postmillennialism was the social correlate of the doctrine of entire sanctification and likewise emphasized the role of human agency and the process of gradual transfer. On the other hand, premillennialism is the social correlate of the doctrine of Holy Spirit baptism, and emphasizes an instantaneous transformation, divine agency, and a human response characterized by tarrying for the "blessed hope.[8]

In the 1860s, concerns about slavery, abolition, and the impending Civil War made life too complex to fit neatly into the postmillennialist schema. These issues jolted its advocates into a sobering reality that required more than they could offer to effectuate the hoped-for millennium. This was taking place in the context of urbanization and industrialization. The burdens of these movements often fell heavily on rural Protestants migrating to the cities out of the Midwest and South. Thus, the postmillennial vision became unthinkable to many.[9]

Though Finney optimistically believed that the preaching of the gospel could end slavery in two years, before the Civil War, the Oberlin Perfectionism school fostered a view of reality that promised more than it could deliver. But the War marked the turning point in the church's hope for changing society. At its end, few, if any, leaders held optimistic views. So "the only way of preserving the millennial hope of imminence was to reconfigure the eschatological vision[10] and place the return of Christ before the millennium as a cataclysmic event.

Belief in the premillennial return of Christ involved more than a question of timing. Its *converts lost hope in man's*

---

[8] Ibid., 165.
[9] Ibid., 160
[10] Ibid.

ability to change this world, since it would be destroyed by Christ's coming. Confidence in man's ability to bring about significant and lasting social progress through the believer's ability to stand up to evil, convert humankind to the faith, or prevent corruption within the church was swept away.[11]

Postmillennialism removed all hope that the Church could make a substantive contribution to the betterment of humankind and emphasized *understanding the times and the nearness of the end.* The new vision and the dominant millennial perspective were shaped by the nineteenth-century British Keswick Movement.[12] This Movement promoted "higher life" teaching that differed from the American Holiness movement's advocacy of "Methodist perfectionism,[13] or "the eradication of the sinful nature. Its leaders felt that such an emphasis "led to trust in self rather than God."

Yet, both groups agreed on the premillennialist vision, and the Keswick Conference introduced the idea of "counter action," meaning that the sinful nature of man was not eradicated or suppressed but was counteracted by many "fillings of the Spirit." Frequent Keswick speaker, Cyrus Ingerson (C. I.) Scofield took that idea and canonized it into doctrine.[14]

The movement facilitated the spread of premillennialism in America via numerous Bible prophecy conferences sponsored by its revivalists, Dwight L. Moody,

---

[11] Prosser, *Dispensationalist Eschatology,* 134.
[12] Ibid. 125
[13] Ibid., 105.
[14] Ibid. 156

Ruben Torrey, A. B. Simpson, Wilbur Chapman, and Bible teachers and convention speakers C. I. Scofield, James M. Gray, and Arthur T. Pierson."[15] It narrowed the spheres in which the church was to be at home."[16] Moody, for example, saw the world as somewhere from which to rescue souls in travail before the second coming of Christ. *It was no longer a milieu to change in preparation for His coming.* Not an inhumane or unconcerned man, Moody despaired of efforts to reform institutions and produce a more just and humane world. He imported prophetic visions of cultural desolation from England and spread them from city to city.[17]

As premillennialists turned their attention to the apocalyptic passages, especially Daniel and Revelation, an elaborate system of prophecies was set up to "rescue these souls.[18] They tried to understand their meanings for the present time and relate the signs of Christ's coming to those who would be saved.[19]

Further, they held that if anything good was to happen in the long term, it would have to come from God, through the return of Christ. Thus, the Church was to attempt to save as many as possible,[20] though there was little hope that many would respond.[21]

---

[15] Ibid., 18-19.
[16] Marty, *Modern American Religion,* 210.
[17] Ibid.
[18] Ibid., 210, 211.
[19] Anderson, *Vision of the Disinherited,* 40.
[20] Marty, *Modern American Religion,* 210.
[21] Ibid., 218.

This left little to do from a social perspective, and the increasing tie to premillennialism exempted those with historical views of the future proposed by Evangelicalism. Frequent predictions of the world's imminent end were made with unwarranted certainty that showed little connection to biblical ideas about being prepared for God's intervention in history. [22]

Dispensationalism

While many Keswick leaders contributed to the spread of premillennial teaching, John Nelson Darby uniquely influenced the impact of dispensational views on Evangelical Protestantism, Holiness revivalism, Fundamentalism, and Pentecostalism.[23] From 1862 through 1877, the controversial founder of the extremely sectarian Plymouth Brethren held Bible conferences throughout the United States and Canada. His intolerant, tyrannical confidence that the Holy Spirit was guiding him in all he taught and did meant that, seemingly, the only way to get along with him was to agree with everything he said.[24] This disposition led to a break with his associate, Benjamin Newton, over teaching regarding the rapture of the church, interpretation of the seventy weeks of Daniel, and the dichotomy between the Jewish and Christian focus of New Testament Scriptures."[25] Yet, his church was puzzled that

---

[22] Ibid.

[23] Prosser, *Dispensationalist Eschatology*, 193.

[24] Ibid., 190.

[25] Ibid., 188.

those who embraced his teaching would not leave their churches and become members of the Plymouth Brethren.[26]

Many premillennialists held a similar dispensational view of history to Darby's philosophy of history that "divided the past into unique eras of God's operation. Both dispensationalism and premillennialism deal with eschatology, or the "last things," for premillennialism is the theological environment in which dispensational eschatology was formed.[27]

Despite problems in Britain, Darby was popular on the Keswick circuit and strongly influenced Moody, who was even more effective in communicating these teachings than Darby himself. Darby taught at Moody conferences on six or seven occasions. During these visits, he introduced the system that, with other issues of prophecy, became a primary subject of discussion.[28] Though Moody had no interest in contributing to pre-tribulationist dispensational premillennialism, he inadvertently absorbed and passed on its *spirit and detail, and* with his death, his Bible Institute refined and promoted Darby and Scofield ideologies.[29]

Darby's system was later popularized by an American theologian, minister, and writer, Cyrus Ingerson Scofield, known for publishing the Scofield Reference Bible in 1909. This version became a foundational text, and the only way for many fundamentalists to understand and interpret the

---

[26] Ibid., 144.
[27] Ibid., 191.
[28] Ibid., 193-195.
[29] Marty, *Modern American Religion,* 223.

Scriptures,[30] and his dispensational system contributed significantly to the African American Apostolic church's worldview.

Scofield's views were not original. Wesley's successor, John Fletcher, used a dispensational scheme to interpret individual spiritual experience and the history of the human race.[31] For him, "dividing both through dispensations of the Father, the Son, and the Holy Spirit."[32] For Fletcher, this emphasis held eschatological importance that came to light in a "posthumously published book entitled *Portrait of St. Paul.* In it, he argued that each dispensation has its correlate promise, proposing dividing both into periods of the Father, the Son, and the Holy Spirit. But since the dispensations also reflect stages in spiritual growth, those living in the era of the Spirit anticipate Christ's coming—even if others ignore it—and actively await the day of God.[33]

Prominent American theologian Charles C. Ryrie, a leading advocate of classical dispensationalism, offered an apologetic for Scofield's eschatology. He lays out the etymology of the term, which appears in the New Testament, pointing out that it was the most effective way to understand the entire Bible.[34]

---

[30] Ibid., 265.

[31] Dayton, *The Theological Roots,* 51-53.

[32] Ibid., 150.

[33] Ibid., 151.

[34] Charles C. Ryrie, *Dispensationalism Today.* Chicago: Moody Press, 1981. See Chapter 1, "Dispensationalism-Help or Heresy?" and Chapter 2, "What is a Dispensation?"

Darby's premillennialism ended when he sought to include the concept of a "pre-tribulation secret "rapture, or "catching away" of the church.[35] He insisted that "the character of the church required that the second coming of Christ be a secret mystery, known only to those who could unlock the Bible's mysteries with the dispensationalist key."[36]

He also introduced the new teaching that the rapture could occur "at any moment."[37] The idea that Daniel's prophecies had been interrupted by the founding of the church and unfulfilled Biblical prophecies would only come to fruition at the rapture,[38] making the Church a "parenthesis Old Testament prophets had not seen." Finally, he held that the events foretold in the Revelation would not occur until after the rapture.[39]

Darby devotee, J. H. Brookes imparted this ideology to Scofield.[40] He had been raised in the Episcopal Church, where dispensationalism was unknown. Scofield was no stranger to evangelicalism. After being won over to dispensationalism by an associate, he became Brookes' student and, within a short time, became a

---

[35] Prosser, *Dispensationalist Eschatology,* 186.

[36] Ibid.

[37] Ibid., 186.

[38] Ibid.,

[39] Ibid. Darby and Newton disagreed over the rapture church. Darby insisted that he got the doctrine from Scriptures. According to Marty and others, the idea of a 'secret Rapture' was prophesied Margaret McDonald, in a charismatic meeting in Scotland, before 1830, See *Modern American Religion,* 222. Darby tried to distance himself from this account and opposed charismatic meetings and expressions of glossolalia.

[40] Marty, *Modern American Religion,* 220.

Congregationalist minister and a featured speaker at Moody's Niagara Bible Conferences.[41] By 1902, his presentations of the "Second Coming of Christ" were so popular that several generous backers supported his ministry. Their support convinced him that the doctrine of the Ages was as essential for understanding Scripture as were clear outlines. Many treated Scofield's outlines almost as though they were the Scriptures themselves.[42]

His system has a numerologist's passion that saw significance in sequences: seven dispensations, seven types of resurrections, eleven mysteries, and eight covenants. Students of his Bible could learn meanings that eighteen centuries of Christian believers had overlooked. His camp convinced itself that this was the true interpretation of Christian scripture.

For Scofield, God rules by different, but clear, principles in various stages of history, some of which occurred within biblical times. What mattered now was the Number Seven, called the "Fullness of Times or the [Reign of God]," when God will "restore the Davidic monarchy in [God's] own person, re-gather dispersed Israel, establish [God's] power over all the earth, and reign one thousand years." Once established, the reign of God would restore divine authority in the earth."[43] This approach to biblical interpretation was the basis for the notes in *Scofield's Bible*.[44] The King James Version was the only Bible most African-

---

[41] Ibid.
[42] Ibid.
[43] Ibid., 221-22.
[44] Ibid., 220.

American Apostolics used from 1919 to the end of the 1950s.

Scofield presents the Church as a "parenthesis" or "interim" to the "two stages promised to the Jews."[45] It is "… a purely spiritual fellowship of true believers distinct from those bodies commonly known as 'churches.'"[46] Furthermore,"… [it] is totally a mystery." For him, even the prophets were in ignorance about this subject. He felt that the key is Israel, and as soon as Israel was back in its own land, God would start the prophetic time clock for the end of the world.[47]

This treatment excludes the Church from the Hebrew Scriptures and the Gospels as only addressed to the Jews who rejected the Kingdom Jesus offered them. Therefore, His teachings are future, having to the millennial kingdom in mind.[48] According to Scofield, "the Gospels do not unfold the doctrine of the Church but, rather, the doctrine to the Israelites; the Epistles are for the Church."[49] Further, Scofield insisted that the teaching in the Gospels relates to Jews' reliance on the Law and not to the Church's reliance on grace. The implication of this teaching can be seen in that the Sermon on the Mount, for example, finds its primary application not to the Church but only to the Jews. "Under the law of the kingdom, for example, no one may hope for forgiveness who has not first forgiven. Under grace, the

---

[45] Prosser, *Dispensationalist Eschatology*, 76.
[46] Ibid., 266.
[47] Ibid., 76-77.
[48] Ibid.
[49] *The Scofield Reference Bible*, 914-15.

Christian is exhorted to forgive because He is already forgiven"... This sermon was addressed to the Jew before the cross and in the coming reign of God. It is, therefore, not now in effect on the Church. This startling view of the Sermon on the Mount as not for the Church but only for the Jews in some future time is essentially the fundamentalist's belief.[50]

Scoffield argues that the Lord's Prayer is not intended for the present age but is instead a legal prayer suited for the future millennium, not the current period of grace. Because it makes divine forgiveness dependent on human forgiveness, some fundamentalists believe it should not be used in church today.[51]

Darby and Scofield's eschatological treatment of the apocalyptic texts of Daniel, Revelation, and Ezekiel[52] renders the Church impotent and indifferent to the contemporary social evils. Its singular concern is to "escape the wrath that is to come..." and assist others in the process. [53]

Fundamentalism

These doctrines are sustained by fundamentalism — the progeny[54] of eschatological dispensationalism and premillennialism, through which dispensationalism made its way into the Holiness and Pentecostal movements.

---

[50] Ibid., 77.

[51] Ibid. This is a reference to James Barr, *Fundamentalism*. Philadelphia: Westminster Press,1978. 193-94.

[52] Ibid., 141.

[53] Ibid., 75.

[54] Ibid., 280.

Fundamentalism emerged during the Moody revivals through his efforts to reach those interested in the prophecies of Scripture and the implications for the Church.[55]

After his death, these conferences took on their own life, and by the time fundamentalism was fully formalized in 1917, the focus had shifted from solely predictive prophecy to popular piety, Bible study and soul-winning. Dispensationalism had replaced premillennialism as the primary emphasis, "and Evangelical churches emphasized the signs of the "end" and the "Second Coming of Christ."[56]

Curtis Lee coined the term "fundamentalism" to describe Christians who followed "the fundamentals of Rueben A. Torrey. His work, *The Fundamentals - A Testimony to the Truth,* written as a series of twelve volumes, set forth the basis of Christian faith in fifteen biblical subjects contained in five major points: the miracles of Christ, the virgin birth (conception) of Christ, the satisfaction view of the atonement, verbal inspiration of the Bible, and the second coming of Christ. [57]

These pamphlets represented a "call to arms" against the influence of" higher criticism" teachings that were sweeping mainline churches and seminaries.[58] So, fundamentalism was a reaction to the influence of

---

[55] See George Marsden, *Fundamentalism and American Culture: The Shaping of the Twentieth-Century Evangelicalism 1870-1925.* New York: Oxford University Press, 1980.

[56] Ibid.

[57] See, R.A. Torrey, A.C. Dixon, et al, editors, *The Fundamentals - A Testimony to the Truth.*

[58] Ibid.

modernity that attempted to recover the teachings that higher criticism rejected.[59] Dispensationalism was a weapon against this modernizing activity, since proponents held that it directly revealed biblical teaching. However, since the structure of fundamentalism was based on Baconian and Scottish common-sense realist views, the new battle was a contest over rationalism. The reactionaries did not have a "fully developed" but rather an "otherwise developed" rationalism.[60]

When one rational system sees itself as the only way of understanding Scripture, there is a repudiation of any other insights. Any deviation from the *only* way of seeing becomes anathema, and heretics are seen everywhere.

Given the popularity of the King James Version of the *Scofield Reference Bible,* and the successful publication and distribution of *The Fundamentals,*[61] the Fundamentalist movement had great influence among the evangelical Protestants, such as pietist and revivalist groups, during the first quarter of the twentieth century. These churches focused more on the apocalyptic texts and the Second Advent than on other portions of Scripture. For them, the end of the world was of more concern than the immediate problems confronting the church and society.[62] The real "damage"… to the church was in their view of contemporary history because it left no room for social or political change.

---

[59] Ibid., 234.
[60] Marty, *Modern American Religion,* 238.
[61] Prosser, *Dispensationalist Eschatology,* 232.
[62] Ibid., 265.

Since each dispensation ended in the failure of [humankind] and God's judgment, it was natural to assume that [humankind] would fail again in this age of "grace." Consequently, the dispensationalists became a self-fulfilling prophecy. In not looking for change, except for the worse, everything around them would naturally tend to get worse. Politically, the signs of the times were especially ominous in the "seething, surging, rioting masses, counter marching with banners on which are emblazoned dynamite, anarchism, communism, nihilism." The end was near.[63]

Through a substantial gift of roughly one million dollars by the Lyman brothers—two Union Oil tycoons—millions of copies of the volumes were distributed. This encouraged the Fundamentalist view that the government had the responsibility to ensure peace and "restrain evil," and not "promote social welfare." Resistance to political involvement left them with fixed on a set of views that had been characteristic of middle-class Americans in the years before the crisis broke. They were frozen in time in a "fin-de-siecle" political frame held over from 1890, and had totally withdrawn from theological thought.[64]

And their "determinist" view of history saw change taking place almost solely through divine intervention that transfers each era into the next.[65] The period from approximately 1900 to 1930, was a time of "great reversal, when adoption of fundamentalism caused most Protestant

---

[63] Ibid., 152.
[64] Ibid., 158.
[65] Ibid., 151, see also Marsden, 58-60.

evangelicals to drop their former social concerns and remove themselves from politics altogether. Those still involved in these areas became progressively more suspect."[66]

The power fundamentalism wielded among the Holiness churches was equally formidable. After all, given the social status of the typical leader of independent Holiness and Pentecostal groups after 1906, it is not surprising that the *Scofield Reference Bible*, *The Fundamentals*, and other such material were read, studied, and taught by most of these groups as absolute truth.[67]

Scofield and his dispensational teachings were unparalleled. It must have seemed to those who first laid their hands on his *Bible that it was* the key to all history, handed down by God himself! For them, it seemed like a whole new book in which, for the first time was clear in its application to history and allowed them to identify with the God who is clearly in control of history in a way that benefits the righteous.[68]

It was equivalent to a chain of meaning in which the geography of the moral imagination excluded the social struggles that both Euro-American evangelicals and African-Americans found unsettling. Euro-American Christians came to understand that biblical passages primarily have meaning in relation to their assigned

---

[66] Ibid. 157.

[67] Ibid., 61.

[68] Douglas Frank, *Less Than Conquerors: How Evangelicals Entered the Twentieth Century.* Grand Rapids, MI: Wm. B. Eerdmans Polishers, 1996, 68.

categories.[69] The effect of this frozen hermeneutic was that the dynamic of an ongoing encounter with Scripture is lost, and the capacity to read Scripture in a way that is personally challenging was largely eliminated.[70]

Beyond the fact that the hermeneutic of Darby, Scofield, and other dispensationalists is excessively tidy, abstract, and limited in its inductive reasoning, their *dispensationalist hermeneutic fosters* disengagement *from the historical struggle between the Church and the world. More importantly, it enables Euro Americans to* overlook significant aspects of history, notably those involving human *suffering.* Further, dispensationalist premillennialism is *a kind of cultural fantasy. For the way Euro-American Christians are taught to read the Bible le*ads them to believe that Christians will not have to suffer.

African-American Apostolics bought into this "cultural fantasy"[71] with only limited benefit. And this has truncated its ability to understand the oppressive reality it faces, and the role it should play in fostering justice and equality.

For as Wilmore pointed out, the Black church, including the African-American Apostolic movement, has been "*seduced* by a foreign evangelical backwardness borrowed from conservative white Christianity."[72] This tragic seduction occurred when the Pentecostal Assemblies of the

---

[69] Michael G. Cartwright, "Wrestling with Scripture: Can Euro-American Christians & African-American Christians Learn to Read Scripture Together?" in Dennis Okholm, *The Gospel in Black & White: Theological Resources for Racial Reconciliation,* Downers Grove, IL: IVP Academic, 1997, 95–112.

[70] Ibid.

[71] Ibid.

[72] Wilmore, "Black Religious Traditions," 297.

World, in fellowship with the Assemblies of God, swallowed whole the fundamentalist dispensationalist ideology that was perceived as the "Only Word of God for True Believers!"

Unfortunately, this thinking was at work in 1914, when several independent Pentecostal churches separated from the Church of God in Christ, headed by black leader Charles Harrison Mason, to form the General Council of the Assemblies of God. Along with the usual Pentecostal article concerning speaking with tongues, the Assemblies insisted that "entire sanctification" should be "earnestly pursued" as a "progressive" rather than an instantaneous experience. The adoption of these statements placed the Assemblies of God outside the Wesleyan tradition and created the first doctrinal divide in the Pentecostal movement.

The new church adopted an essentially congregational or "Baptistic" form of government, while earlier southern groups had developed episcopal or "Methodist" forms.[73] Its Constitution became the model for subsequent "finished work" denominations that coalesced after 1914. With the Pentecostal movement divided almost equally between the advocates of the second work and the finished work," the Assemblies became the largest Finished Work denomination, and the hope of unifying all Pentecostalists was forfeited.[74]

The Scofield Bible had sold over two million copies by that time, and Pentecostals generally supported it and most

---

[73] Ibid.
[74] Ibid. Ibid., 153-156.

Fundamentalist teaching. According to Marty, they were at home with dispensationalism and coalesced with the growing Fundamentalist party. They rejected much of modernity and all of modernism, but Pentecostals insisted that theirs was the movement of the Spirit for the new age.[75]

Thus, Pentecostals and Fundamentalists had a "close but tangential"[76] relationship based on their reliance on the Scofield Bible. Fundamentalist articles and the Scofield Bible formed the core of Pentecostal theology[77] with added emphasis on the Holy Spirit's presence and work in the church. But despite Pentecostals' reliance on dispensational perspectives of Fundamentalist literature, Fundamentals did not hold the same respect for them. They "despised Pentecostalists for their sectarianism, enthusiasm... and worship of spiritual "gift" which they held no longer existed.[78] Pentecostals were "seldom welcome... as allies of Fundamentalists or called... into their councils."[79]

Pentecostals and Fundamentalists shared a connection through the Scofield Bible, which shaped Pentecostal theology alongside their focus on the Holy Spirit. However, Fundamentalists did not accept Pentecostals due to their sectarianism and emphasis on spiritual gifts, rarely considering them allies or including them in their discussions.

---

[75] Marty, *Modern American Religion*, 247.
[76] Ibid.
[77] Prosser, 251.
[78] Ibid., 160.
[79] Ibid., 251.

Lacking its own theology, the Pentecostal movement "grafted itself onto an alien doctrine." But, this uncritical embrace of the Fundamentalist agenda proved to be devastating to black Pentecostal self-interest and raised serious problems for their hermeneutical, sociological, historical, and political identity."[80]

Since dispensationalism's influence became "embedded in official Pentecostal doctrine,"[81] when the split over the new issue took place, the Assembly of God took its orientation with them.[82] When the Oneness faction formed the Pentecostal Assemblies of the World later that year,[83] it uncritically made the Scofieldian worldview its own.

Fundamentalism has dominated American evangelical theology since the mid--nineteenth century."[84] Yet, according to Prosser, the unity of the fundamentalist movement did not come as much from a core belief in the Bible as from a Baconian ideal and Scottish commonsense realism. In this scheme, the history of the church was

---

[80] Ibid., 282

[81] Ibid., 261.

[82] Synan, *The Holiness Pentecostal,* 158. This issue had to do with a 'revelation' that several leaders received regarding the appropriate baptism of believers. It was first introduced at a camp meeting in California where it was stated that the proper formula for baptism was in the name of Jesus Christ, according to Acts 2:38. Many of the members of the Assembly of God accepted the 'revelation' and were rebaptized. But when they insisted that everyone be rebaptized and the teaching regarding the Godhead be changed to what became known as Oneness or Unitarian that the councils led to this major split."

[83] Reed, *Dictionary,* 650.

[84] Ibid., 168. According to Marty this Baconian System which first gathers the teachings of the Word of God, then seeks to deduce some general law upon which those facts can be arranged. See his *Modern American Religion,* 221.

interpreted through artificially unified "facts" as well as biblical laws.[85]

Princeton theologians Charles Hodge, Archibald Alexander Hodge, B. B. Warfield, and John Gresham Machen fought against the forces of modernism as a threat to the orthodox Christian faith. They took on the higher criticism by proffering doctrines of the inerrancy and the infallibility of Scripture. With their perceived courageous commitment to the "defense of the faith,"[86] the Fundamentalists were attractive to the early Pentecostals. Even now, those who question their work are considered worldly or backslidden.

Yet, their teaching questioned the legitimacy of the Pentecostal experience and demonized expressions central to the Pentecostal corpus. So, the wedding of dispensationalism and Pentecostalism created a 'hybrid'[87] theology that limits Pentecostals' capacity to respond to the Holy Spirit and use spiritual gifts to engage in the struggle for justice. The African-American Apostolic church has so closely followed dispensational ideology *and "last days" theology* so totally that it has failed in its responsibility to work for justice. This has *led to a passive acceptance of evil precisely because that evil may seem to be leading to a complete breakdown of society, ushering in the reign of God.* This theology comprises some of the most visible elements of the Pentecostal tradition. By adopting the more hopeful holiness/Pentecostal tradition found among other blacks

---

[85] Ibid.
[86] Prosser, 241-242.
[87] Ibid., 287. Prosser refers to it as an 'Alien Theological System.'

and Hispanics, the movement could see the gifts of the Spirit active in the present social, political, and spiritual life, not just in the past or in the future.[88]

The African American Apostolic worldview is hybridized from two theological concepts that are the antithesis of each other—dispensationalism and the free operation or liberating power of the Holy Spirit. These forces are not the only reason for its lack of participation in social action. But "as a [person] thinketh in [his/her] heart so is [he/she],"[89] and since ideas shape behavior, much of what the Church does comes from its understanding of God's work in the world, and its felt connection with that work, and what God has called the Church into existence to do.

The adoption of a Dispensationalist worldview carries significant responsibility for its disengagement. A primary distinction between dispensationalist fundamentalism and Pentecostalism is their view of the church. Fundamentalists see the church as a purely spiritual and heavenly entity that plays no role in addressing issues of social change or injustice. They see much of biblical prophecy as irrelevant for today and consider charismatic gifts, particularly glossolalia, as intended only for the Apostolic age.

In contrast, Pentecostals maintain that the gifts of the Spirit remain active today, citing events like the Azusa Revival as evidence. But their single focus on personal salvation produces an inward-facing faith that neglects the

---

⁸⁸ Ibid., 288-289.
⁸⁹ Proverbs 23:7

movement's prophetic voice and fails to challenge unjust systems. While acts of charity may be present, the broader call to justice—rooted in Scripture and exemplified by the early church's engagement with the oppressed—is diminished, leaving structural inequities largely unaddressed and perpetuating a cycle in which faith is divorced from social responsibility.

Chapter IV

Taking Agency for Social Transformation

Taking agency for social transformation means exercising authority, influence, or power to bring about desired conditions within society. It is taking responsibility to help shape society according to one's principles and values, moving from passively awaiting spiritual deliverance, to purposely acting as salt and light in the world. Agency is demonstrated not only through private devotion, but also by addressing community challenges and promoting justice and compassion. Jesus' sacrifice was for the whole world[1] not just those who would respond to the proclamation of the Gospel and agree to be saved. Following His command, the church is called to impact a morally and spiritually troubled world for which He died.

The disciples were never led to believe that obeying His commands would be easy, but the urgency of the task was clear. According to John, Jesus warned that in carrying it out, they would have tribulation. He assured them that though their efforts would be resisted, they would be fruitful, and encouraged them that He had "overcome the world."[2] While the movement's eschatology often found its roots in the Scofieldian dispensational future-oriented expectation of the Lord's return, it must move beyond

---

[1] John 3:16.
[2] See John 16:33.

passive anticipation of deliverance and embrace an active, transformative role within society. It must deliberately reexamine inherited theological frameworks and reconsider mission as a dynamic engagement with the world's challenges, not as withdrawal or isolation. This scripturally shaped vision and prioritization of robust religious education will allow it to more faithfully embody the calling to be a catalyst for holistic social and spiritual renewal.

In the past, uncritical acceptance of *Scofield's* triumphalism as superior Scripture interpretation limited its witness. Emphasis on dispensational premillennialism and "end-time" events permeated its teaching and colored its perspective on how daily life should be lived.[3] All too often, parishioners' response to oppression has been, "I'll be glad when the Rapture comes, and we can get out of here!"[4] Yet, though the New Testament teaches the Lord's imminent return, and the disciples anticipated the event, salvation history shows that Jesus never intended passive waiting. Instead, he expected active engagement and purpose. He wanted the church to *be [His] witnesses in Jerusalem and in all Judaea, and in Samaria, and unto the uttermost part of the earth,"* and empowers them to do so.[5] For he tells the disciples, *"It is not for you to know times or*

---

[3] Prosser, *Dispensationalist Eschatology*, 245.

[4] This is a common saying among African American Apostolics when crimes are committed within the community, or statistics are announced on the rising all Judea and Samaria and to the end of the earth. (RSV.

[5] Acts 1:8

seasons which... [God] has fixed by [God's] own authority. But you shall receive power when the Holy Spirit has come upon you.

Moreover, He commands them to... *make disciples of all the nations, and teach them to observe everything He commanded.*[6] Since the church's perception of God, its understanding of divine self-revelation, and the relationship between God, humanity, nature, sin, and evil informs its engagement with the world, Scofieldian dispensationalists have apparently overlooked a significant aspect of that initial communication.

As the African American Apostolic church wrestles with its mission, it must tackle some important questions. Will it seclude itself from the world with no interaction beyond what is necessary? Will it become an island in a sea of evil, while awaiting its ultimate salvation at the *Parousia?* Should it continue to present itself as the only true expression of God's church and resist ecumenical involvement with other religious expressions that do not conform to its model?[7]

None of these answers is acceptable, for Jesus explicitly cautioned that salt that has lost its taste" it should be discarded and trampled on. And while calling His disciples to be the light of the world, He cautioned that a city must be set on a hill, and a lamp must be on a stand to be of benefit.[8] So, the church's presence should make a radical

---

[6] See Matthew 28: 19-20. (The Geneva Study Bible) .

[7] This may sound a bit far-fetched but conversations around these themes occur quite frequently in ministerial gatherings and at Diocese Conferences and Convocations.

[8] Matthew 5:13-16.

difference in the world. Though some perceive active social consciousness and concern for social justice as "worldly," the *African American Apostolic* church must respond to this challenge."[9] For the Law and the prophets link knowledge of God to the pursuit of justice and defense of the poor.

The "reign of God" is a central focus in Jesus' preaching. This reign is not purely personal, apolitical, inward, or other-worldly hope. Such an understanding undermines the significance of Jesus' ministry. Though sometimes mistaken for Christian orthodoxy, the notion that Christianity is primarily a religion of personal salvation is a modern one. Considerable patristic writing relates prayer and social action, and the orthodox tradition has always rejected the false dichotomy between personal and social, rooting its concern *with the inward in a materialistic and socially based theology.* Hence, the stress throughout the tradition is on the social dimensions of the liturgy.[10] To grasp the church's role in society, we must broaden our understanding of church history and apply a more critical hermeneutic. For seeking to practice "authentic piety" that brings bout significant social change requires a radical *metanoia.*"[11]

---

[9] This is a common expression among most Pentecostals. It means one's interests are too focused on what is taking place in the world. It is also used to describe those who take in cultural activities that are not condoned by the church.

[10] Kenneth Leech "Spirituality and Social Justice" in Chelsy Jones, Geoffrey Wainwright and Edward Yarnold, eds., *The Study of Spirituality.* New York: Oxford University Press, 1986, 584.

[11] Ibid.

Faithfulness to the Lord's command to become a change agent requires two things: First, an investment of time and resources to rethink its worldview and embrace God's vision of reality and its place within it. Secondly, a commitment by leaders to encourage involvement in the vocation of religious teaching and leadership. Without replacing the important role of proclamation, this emphasis and the allocation of resources must move from the margins to the center and be accorded the requisite support.[12]

Reshaping the African Church's World View and Mission

The African American Apostolic church's vision of reality is primarily the same as other theistic worldviews: The sovereign and transcendent God made humankind in God's image to worship, praise, and serve God. They generally share key Pentecostal theological commitments—such as salvation, Holy Spirit baptism, divine healing, and belief in the Second Coming of Christ. Its emphasis on the Rapture differs from mainline beliefs and has implications for human relationships as well. For though one should "... love (one's) neighbor as (one's self)... "[13] one is to "keep oneself unspotted from the world,"[14] " ... come out from among the unsaved and be separate from them, and touch

---

[12] Thomas H. Groome, Christian *Religious Education: Sharing Our Story and Vision.* New York: HarperCollins Publishers, 1980, 49-51.

[13] Matthew 22: 19.

[14] James 1: 27.

nothing unclean...”[15] This emphasis minimizes contact with the world, lest one might compromise readiness to go back with Christ when He returns at any moment to receive his church.[16] Finally, followers believe the Holy Spirit will “lead into all truth,” rendering secular or cultural sources questionable.[17] In a largely Fundamentalist, Dispensationalist understanding, a distinction is made regarding activities of the Holy Spirit. While Pentecostals celebrate *glossolalia* and the *charismata*, Fundamentalists contend that such supernatural works ceased with the end of the Apostolic Era.

Mary Boys’ “Matrix for Analysis of the Classic Expressions of Religious Education” provides a lens to closely examine the role of religious education in the African American Apostolic church.[18] It highlights how faith education historically results from the intersection of a particular theological perspective with a specific educational outlook.”[19] The matrix includes ten “Foundational Questions,” five of which explore the meaning of religion, five of which explore the meaning of faith-based education: Evangelism, Religious Education, Christian Education, and Catholic Education.[20] Although the African American Apostolic church does not fit snugly into the Boys categories, it most closely resembles the

---

[15] 2 Cor. 6:17.
[16] John 14:1-3; Acts 1:8 and I Thessalonians 4: 13-17.
[17] Dayton, *The Theological Roots of Pentecostalism*, 22.
[18] Boys, *Educating in Faith*, 9.
[19] Ibid., 8.
[20] See Boys, 39, 66, 80, and 111. Boys includes a fifth expression titled ‘Contemporary Modifications of the Classic Expressions’.

Evangelical view. The matrix reveals why a formal religious education program is vitally important in changing this worldview and helping it become the change agent that Jesus Christ has called it to be.

Expressions of the African American Apostolic Church

Foundational Questions	African American Apostolic Expressions

Foundational Questions	African American Apostolic Expressions
REVELATION How is God revealed? What is the significance of worship?	+ Primacy of revelation accorded to scripture
	+ God's Word meant to "crush" and "crack" the stony heart through the preached Word
	* The Holy Spirit is present to "illuminate" believers to the meaning of scripture if they study *(i.e., personal devotions)*. See John 14:26; 16:12ff and I John 2:26-27
	+ Embraces Fundamentalist emphasis on the inerrancy of the character of the scripture
CONVERSION What constitutes the spirit of conversion: What is the role of psychology?	+ Conversion of the affections is stressed: "A change of heart, not opinions"
	* Conversion seen as a "crisis event" that occurs in three stages that can be collapsed into one moment: (1) repentance, (2) water baptism, and (1) baptism in the Holy Spirit with the "initial evidence of speaking with tongues
	+ Preaching engenders personal decisions to give oneself to Christ
	+ The Mission of leading others to Christ is primary and urgent
	* Psychology is not considered an aspect of conversion
FAITH & BELIEF What is faith? How are faith and belief related?	* Creeds are rejected as unnecessary - the Bible is taken as its creed
	* The affective dimension of faith is everything
	* Any attention to the cognitive is informal or minimal in most instances. This is beginning to change in both the COOLJC and the PAW as they've started Bible Colleges and Bible Institutes and are seeking accreditation for the former
	+ Faith is developed from preachings, personal Bible study and devotions via audio and video tapes marketed by TV Evangelists, *et al*
	+ Fundamentalist emphasis on truth as propositional. Use of C.I. Scofield Reference notes, "Rightly Dividing the Word of Truth." "Jesus is Coming," Clarence Larkins' Illustrative work in Revelations
	* Writings by PAW and COOLJC founders, G.T. Haywood and R.C. Lawson, are considered authoritative, next to the scriptures

THEOLOGY What is the role of theology?	*	Approved Apostolic Doctrine, not theology, receives most emphasis, though some, but not many, leaders, use other materials
	*	Theology of experience prevalent in most traditions
	*	Memorization of dispensational pre-millennial system required for ordination of ministers, and is the standard for preaching and teaching
	+	Armenian emphasis is dominant
	+	The few "learned" ministers who endeavor to improve themselves educationally are viewed with suspicion
FAITH AND CULTURE How does faith situate one in the world? An uncompromising counter-cultural stance	+	Distinction made between supernatural and natural
	*	Christ against culture stance
	*	Direction of the culture renounced, while there is accommodation to its consumerist impulses and emphasis on individualism
CURRICUUM & TEACHING What methods are in place?	+	Teaching is essentially transmissive
	*	The banking system of teaching is used
	*	Bible Institute curriculum oriented to biblical literacy and doctrinal accuracy as put forth by founders or most articulate persons in the organization
	*	Sunday school and Bible study groups are only formal teaching agencies, except for the Bible Institute and College
	*	Strongest emphasis is still on evangelism and Pastoral ministry in the five (5) Bible institutes
	*	Limited emphasis on education overall
	*	Lack the transforming power that would make them relevant to the well-being of society
	*	Eschatology prohibits political or social engagement since Jesus may return "at any time" to take the Church and establish his Kingdom after the Great Tribulation
	*	A "Christ against culture" posture is function of its eschatological perspective

Foundational Questions	African American Apostolic Expressions
KNOWLEDGE	* Knowledge linked to conversion
What does it mean to know?	* Knowledge is a function of charismata made possible through the operation of the Holy Ghost in the believer's life
How is it more than comprehending information?	* One gains knowledge through the charismata[1] and the preaching and teaching office Christ gave the Church[2]
What is the relationship between knowing and doing?	
SOCIAL SCIENCES	* Limited Use of psychology by pastoral counselors
How formative a role should social sciences play?	* Developmental counseling is taught as part of the Bible Institute curriculum and the Bible College curriculum, Evangelical Teacher's Association (ETA)
What is the role of psychology?	* Introductory courses to psychology, being taught in the Bible College

+ Evangelism.

* Statements unique to AA.AP Church.

---

[1] II Cor. 12:14

[2] Eph. 4:11

Chapter V

The Role of Religious Education

This matrix reveals a great deal about the influence of religious education in the African American Apostolic church. Aside from Bible institutes and general Bible classes taught for an hour or so on Wednesdays or Fridays by the pastor or ministers, there is no formal program of religious education. Other Christian education efforts are put forth by "church mothers" teach the women[3] and conduct Bible classes. Or a missionary department that sponsors services for women to speak on various topics.[4]

W. L. Bonner College was organized in 1996, as a four-year Bible school to strengthen religious education and received accreditation by the International Christian Accrediting. Association[5] and Applicant Status with the American Association of Bible Colleges, but deferred pursuing full accreditation from the Association for Biblical Higher Education, though this would have been a historic achievement among Apostolic Pentecostal institutions.

Aside from these efforts, the local Sunday School is the closest program to a formal religious education, but this has declined. Classes typically share spaces with little

---

[3] R. C. Lawson, "The Ministry of Women in the Church" *The Contender for the Faith,* April 1958, 11-15.

[4] This is especially the case with African American Apostolic churches such as COOLJC that don't ordain women nor license them to serve as Evangelists. T

[5] An accrediting agency for Christian schools that was formed by the Oral Roberts University Educational Fellowship

separation, and teachers often lack the training Boys explicitly calls for.[6]

A faith community's capacity to bear effective witness is tied to ongoing transformation.[7] If traditions are taught as mere indoctrination,[8] their transformative impact will be diminished or lost, [9] and educators will be unable to illuminate these traditions or enrich the community's understanding of them."[10]

These traditions are not ends in themselves but lead to the community's renewal. They are not merely for maintenance but should enable the community to recognize God's involvement with its creation and call it to ongoing conversion. Otherwise, traditions become idols.[11]

If we fail to recognize this point, indoctrination replaces education, fails to foster   liberation,[12] and brings spiritual and moral bondage.[13] Doctrine becomes lifeless ideas that fail to guide us on how to engage them. So, they forfeit the transformation that continual personal and communal conversion brings.[14] The reality of the Lord's return is certain, but the church must determine what to do in the meantime and how religious education contributes to shaping its mission.

---

[6] Boys, *Educating in Faith,* 196.

[7] Ibid., 210.

[8] Paulo Freire, *Pedagogy of the Oppressed.* Myra Bergman Ramos, Trans. New York: Continuum, 1992, 57-58.

[9] Boys, *Educating in Faith*, 209.

[10] Ibid.

[11] Ibid., 203.

[12] Ibid., 210.

[13] Ibid., 199.

[14] Ibid., 203.

For theologian and religious educator, Thomas Groome, the reign of God is central to our understanding of faith and cannot be reduced to a 'place for souls later on.'"[15] In the Hebrew tradition, this reign signifies God establishing sovereignty in concrete activity in history.[16]

This is not the authoritarian rule of a capricious God. Instead, a caring, trustworthy God intervenes in history to transform the present order and bring creation to fullness, where nature is wholly and wondrously transformed, and the serenity of Paradise is renewed."[17] Thus, in the fulfillment of God's reign, every human yearning will be fully realized; law, justice, peace, wholeness, happiness, and freedom will characterize its every expression.[18]

Since this reign is already a reality, Yahweh expects Israel to honor its covenant, living according to God's intentions." Yahweh expects Yahweh's people to respond to what has been provided for them by releasing those bound unjustly, untying yokes, setting the oppressed free, sharing bread with the hungry, sheltering the oppressed and the homeless, clothing the naked, and not neglecting those in need. [19]

Jesus had this vision in mind in preaching the reign of God as his central theme.[20] For there is scarcely a page of the Synoptic gospels that does not reference it. Mark recounts that after John's arrest, "Jesus appeared in Galilee

---

[15] Ibid.
[16] Ibid., 36.
[17] Ibid., 37. See Isa. 35:1-10.
[18] Ibid.
[19] Ibid. See Isa. 58:6-7.
[20] Ibid., 39.

proclaiming the good news of God: "This is the time of fulfillment. The (reign of God) is at hand! Reform your lives and believe in the gospel." From that opening announcement the reign of God was Jesus' constant theme.[21]

In maintaining continuity with his Hebrew heritage, Jesus portrayed the reign of God as a dynamic, concrete reality, pointing to God's saving action as the embodiment "of God's will in history." Yet, though this Hebrew understanding is central to Jesus' teaching, He considered it fully present in his person, work and ministry.[22]

Jesus radicalizing the message, including the love commandment as the supreme element. Although not foreign to the Jewish tradition, Jesus' emphasis on the commandment to love one's neighbor is rooted in Jewish tradition, he makes it an especially prominent and powerful requirement for anyone who would participate in the reign of God. For He insisted that one cannot love God without loving one's neighbor and removed all limits on who is "my neighbor.[23] Thus, theologian, Gustaf Aulen observes that when Jesus calls people to fellowship with him, he calls them to service in the world,"… as his fellow worker in the service of men."[24]

Participation in the reign of God is not a passive experience. Recipients of God's actions are called to actively live in partnership and service to one another. For Jesus

---

[21] Ibid.

[22] Ibid.

[23] Ibid., 40-41.

[24] Ibid. See Gustaf Aulen's Jesus *in Contemporary Historical Research.* Translated by Ingalill H. Hjelm. Philadelphia: Fortress Press, 1976, 144.

proclamation is both a symbol of hope in God's saving power that will ultimately bring all things under divine sovereignty and a call to action that requires our response. Therefore, it summons us to align with God's will, which demands a transformation of heart and a commitment to love our neighbor.[25]

The church's communication must be centered in the work and teaching of Jesus, as a "reclamation of the earliest tradition"[26] Its urgency stems from an essential link between preaching Jesus as Lord and Savior and preaching the reign of God. Preaching Jesus as the Christ requires that we preach what Jesus preached—the reign of God. So, the symbol must be recentered in our understanding of what it means to live a Christian life and become our primary purpose for religious education.

Contemporary theologians recognize the importance of this "eschatological dimension of the Christian message" and set about to deconstruct a purely otherworldly connotation that serves the interests of the oppressors at the expense of their victims. Liberation "theologians (including black womanist theologians) insist that Christian theology must arise out of a context of *active participation in society on behalf of the values of God's (reign)."*[27]

This understanding suggests a role for religious education in communicating the nature of God's reign. For its role is to facilitate the development of Christian lives,[28] so they may be lived in accordance with the demands of the

---

25 Ibid., 41.
26 Ibid., 42
27 Ibid., 43.
28 Ibid., 34.

reign of God. Its function is not to prepare believers for a sudden escape, nor to keep them in isolation from the world, but equip them for spiritually potent lives reflecting the character of Jesus who embodied the reign of God and thus transformed his society and the world.[29]

Role of the Christian Educator

Christian educators with this attitude would be potent instruments for the transformation of the church, their communities and their world. Boys underscores the role of the educator as 'a catalyst of transformation.'[30] Their role is making the religious community's traditions accessible, while connecting traditions and transformation.[31] Religious education is the medium by which the members of the community gain a right understanding, under the right conditions, of traditions which are believed to be true. This enables us to continually experience the powerful transformation that tradition evokes.[32] In Boys' view, traditions are a storehouse from which a community shapes its self-understanding. It selects traditions as sources for survival and growth amidst new realities. The changed context stimulates rethinking the past. What happened before thus lies open to numerous possible understandings. The past is always open and never finished.[33]

---

29 Ibid., 50.
30 Ibid., 203.
31 Ibid., 193.
32 Ibid., 210.
33 Ibid., 196.

In bringing about transformation in the church's "the past is always open and never finished."[34] Its traditions must be complemented and enriched by insights from present religious and secular scholarship.[35] Accommodating this process opens the church to unimagined possibilities.

Redesigning Structures for a New Vision

The church must adjust to fit it for the new tasks that this new understanding of the responsibility to *teach* men and women "... to observe all that the Lord... commanded."[36] Again, this includes more than evangelistic outreach and the 'priestly functions,'[37] that are the prevailing focus of the church. It also involves being in the world as advocates for justice, peace, and liberation.[38]

This rethinking of God's activity among us requires reordering priorities and resources so that the church's stewardship brings glory to God.[39] This is not a simple undertaking, given the church's history of primarily celebrating the preaching ministry. But it is vitally necessary if the church is to *fully engage in the* challenge of the twenty-first century.

---

[34] Ibid. .

[35] Ibid., 192-213. Boys" discussion of the components of her definition of the role of religious education is instructive, yet challenging for this work within the African American Apostolic tradition.

[36] See Matthew 28: 20b.

[37] Lincoln and Mamiya, *The Black Church,* 12.

[38] Ibid.

[39] Matthew 5: 16.

The First Line of Action

Lawrence Cremin's perspectives on education offer insight into how the vision of the church in educating members about the reign of God has to take first priority.[40] He defines education as the result of the direct or indirect, intended or unintended, deliberate, systematic, and sustained effort to transmit, evoke, or acquire knowledge, values, attitudes, skills, and sensibilities. His *definition calls attention to the wide range of situations and institutions in which education has gone forward.*[41]

The church is among those "situations and institutions"[42] that by the very nature of its activities is engaged in providing an educational experience for its members, whether it knows it or not,[43] or plans to provide educational instruction.[44]

Leaders must cultivate awareness regarding educational activity to enable conscious and deliberate change.[45] According to Robert Pazmino, educational structures, including social agencies and organizations whose primary role involves reforming and imparting knowledge, values, and culture to subsequent generations,

---

[40] Groome, *Religious education,* 50.

[41] Cremin, 10. See also Robert W. Pazmino, *Principles & Practices of Christian Education: An Evangelical Perspective.* Grand Rapids, MI: Baker Book House, 1992, 62.

[42] Ibid.

[43] In this case it may be miseducation. This is even more reason for the church being cognizant of what is taking place to avoid the negative results.

[44] In many Pentecostal and Charismatic churches, during the 'praise and worship' segment of the service, singers and musicians lead the congregation in extolling love of God and thanksgiving for God's faithfulness through scripturally based songs. Still, many African American Pentecostals 'devotional services' resemble the early movement, resisting the new approach as lacking spontaneity.

[45] See Pazmino, *Principles,* 59-89.

are essential for preserving the continuity of its social life.

Individuals may engage in self-directed learning and independently interact with these structures to pursue personal development. Yet even those not usually active in settings are influenced by others.[46] Even a 'couch potato' is influenced to some degree by the media that constitutes structure.[47] According to Pazmino's reading of Brazilian educator Paulo Freire's concept of 'conscientization,'[48] every society makes an impact on its members. Learning experiences. People learn together, for "learning 'implicitly or explicitly' involves others.[49] Pazmino argues that self-initiated, self-directed learning can only happen when a 'teachable spirit' is in place. Finally, that life and work are connected, and the way the Creator, Redeemer, and Sustainer exist together serves as an example of social or communal life for us. Being made in God's image and living as part of God's creation requires mutual awareness and recognition of how spiritual and ecological life are interconnected.[50]

When discussing the nature of educational structures, three categories of educational experiences must be taken into consideration: formal, informal, and nonformal.[51]

---

[46] Ibid., 59.

[47] Ibid., 60.

[48] See Freire, *Pedagogy of the Oppressed*, 19. The term *conscientization* refers to learning to perceive social, political, and economic contradictions, and act against the oppressive elements of reality. Pazmino notes that Noel E. McGinn uses the term "problem-posing" or "transforming education," given the Western tendency to divorce action from consciousness-raising. Freire relates education to personal and corporate activity in the world to transform those realities that don't promote human freedom.

[49] Pazmino, 60

[50] Ibid. 60-61.

[51] Ibid.

Formal education refers to structured, institutionalized learning, usually organized by age or level, from preschool to higher education. Informal education involves lifelong learning, gained through daily experiences and interactions. Nonformal education occurs outside these systems and targets specific groups for particular skills or knowledge. The key difference between the categories lies in motivation, goals, structure, and flexibility of approach.[52]

Formal education emphasizes content and systematic instruction through schooling. Nonformal education focuses on the community or society, especially the socialization and formation of members in a community or society. Informal education emphasizes the daily, routine experiences that provide occasions for discovery and self-education.[53]

These insights help identify the structures that influence educational experiences within the church and allow us to determine how to employ them to create a transformative climate for learning. The structures include the family, the community, the economy, social agencies, the church, the media, the school and the body politic.[54]

Recommendations for Change

Pazmino's presentation argues that, like society, churches have organizational structures shaped by political interests that can either strengthen or weaken the church's unity and interdependence.

---

[52] Ibid., 62-63.

[53] Ibid., 65.

[54] Ibid., 65-88. This section offers greater clarity of the nature of the influence and challenges of these structures.

African American churches are generally organized along ecclesiastical lines that include several jurisdictional regions, dioceses, districts and individual congregations.[55] The denominations are rich with talent and the number of those with formal education or professional training is increasing. This climate creates a golden opportunity to propose a program to prepare its members for "lived Christian lives."[56] This proposal should focus on equipping the organization to proactively address the long-neglected issues of social justice, equality, racism, and sexism.

Though organizational commitment is strong, some crucial adjustments will make the church a viable witness in the world in the twenty-first century. Governing bodies of organizations like the Board of Apostles is the Church of Our Lord Jesus Christ,[57] cannot develop its vision and mission in isolation from the talent and gifts of the men and women who support them.

This calls for reflecting on its prior work, and the twenty-first-century challenges and restating the organization's mission and the vision grounded in an appropriate understanding of the Lord's command to his disciples in Matthew 5:13-16. The hard task of reevaluating eschatological understandings should include a commitment to deal with social and political problems. To do less is to align ourselves with those that say they are

---

[55] See the *Discipline Book, The Church of Our Lord Jesus Christ of the Apostolic Faith, Inc.* 6th edition, 1991. New York: Office of The Executive Secretary, 1961, 31.

[56] Groome, *Religious Education.* 140.

[57] I use the COOLJC, the organization with which I am most familiar as a model of what is possible if African American Apostolic churches adopted this or a similar proposal to complement a strong religious education program.

concerned about the souls of men but,... are not with the slums that damn them, the economic conditions that strangle them, and the social conditions that cripple them." For Martin Luther King, Jr. characterizes such a position as being "dry as dust."[58]

Reflecting on mission to create a plan should help leaders understand the magnitude and complexity of this work. As organizational leaders investigate the various "educational programs" already being offered by the various groups. The activities conducted by these groups are what Pazmino defines as nonformal educational programs.[59]

A Curriculum that reflects the issues and concerns that are unique to the participants must be developed. Further, greater awareness and appreciation must be created regarding how other Pentecostal groups and non-Pentecostal traditions helped shape our present understanding.

The Board of Education should develop a concrete plan to expose leaders and workers to pedagogies that can enrich teaching and learning experiences, while, at the same time, releasing the liberatory power that has been too long absent in many of these activities. Christian education consultants and teachers could present workshops and seminars at existing major meetings since they are generally well attended by a good cross section of members. Such presentations might serve the dual purpose of enhancing

---

[58] Scott-King, *The Words.* 148.
[59] Pazmino, *Principles,* 63.

the potential impact of such events and increasing attendance.

Shared Christian Praxis: Some Definitions

The African American Apostolic Church is an example of a tradition that faces serious theological challenges. For, if the critique of dispensationalism is valid, the challenge is to replace it without reducing the urgency in its witness. How might this shift affect the church's understanding of its mission? Could other theological frameworks—such as Evangelical, Neo-Evangelical, or Black Holiness-Pentecostal traditions with premillennialist perspectives—better address the gospel's social dimensions? These challenges. allow us to revisit the genesis of its doctrines and traditions, potentially strengthening their relevance. Effectively addressing them requires leadership equipped with theological training Groome's "Shared Christian Praxis" approach addresses the more pertinent question of what educational approach best informs these ideas.[60]

Education

For Groome, education as "... an activity of leading out" with three points of emphasis: 1) a point from which it begins, 2) a present process, and 3) a future toward which the 'leading out' is focused."[61] He describes the educational activity as a political act that engages people with their present, connects them to a heritage, and opens possibilities

---

[60] Thomas H. Groome, *Religious Education,* 184-231.

[61] Groome notes that the etymology of the word is a clue to the nature of the activity. The English word comes from the Latin '*ducare*' meaning 'to lead,' with the prefix *e,* meaning 'out,' so education is an activity of leading out

for individuals and communities. As such, it should help learners critically reclaim their past to shape their present and future. His use of the term 'pilgrims in time' points to the idea that people connect with their past and embrace 'systems and artifacts that support them in being together.' They share a "common past" and are not, "aimless, wandering individuals." For him, people's stories, discoveries, customs, myths, symbols, rituals, artifacts, systems, institutions, skills, etc., provide a present out of which to shape a future. The educator's role is ensuring that the heritage of the past pilgrimage is not lost, but is intentionally remembered and made available to the present to maintain its 'ongoingness.' For both the present and the past must be involved in creatively transforming the learner toward an open future.[62]

For Groom, education has an 'already 'being realized,' and 'not yet' dimension, separated only for the "sake of analysis" but not in practice.[63] The "already" dimension pertains to either the learner's existing knowledge or the educator's understanding of what the learner is innately capable of assimilating. The second dimension shifts focus from pre-existing knowledge to what the learner uncovers as new insights that emerge through ongoing discovery. The third dimension signifies the future-oriented aspect of educational guidance. Leading such learning mut be an intentional activity aimed toward what is possible for human knowledge to achieve.[64]

---

[62] Ibid. 14-15.
[63] Ibid.
[64] Ibid., 21.

Christian Religious Education

Adding the word "Christian" to this definition, distinguishing it from other forms of religious education.[65] For the "human quest for the transcendent in which one's relationship with an ultimate ground of being is brought to consciousness and somehow given expression."[66] He sees Christian religious education as an intentional activity that engages with individuals on their spiritual journey, focusing on God's work in the present, the narrative of the Christian faith community, and the vision of God's reign, whose foundations are already evident among us.[67]

The Purpose of Religious Education

The overarching purpose of Christan religious education is to "enable people to live …lives of Christian faith."[68] The biblical symbol of the "reign of God is the ultimate hermeneutical principle that best expresses this telos. It should be the primary guideline for what to teach from the tradition, how to teach it, and the direction of its politics. Promoting God's rule in people's lives calls for educating for the wholeness of human freedom…[69] So primarily, this education is not a personal and private event, but a means of "forming people to be historical

---

[65] Ibid., 2.

[66] Ibid., 22.

[67] Ibid., 25.

[68] Ibid., 34.

[69] Thomas H. Groome, *Sharing Faith: A Comprehensive Approach to Religious Education & Pastoral Ministry. The Way of Shared Praxis.* New York, New York: Harper Collins, 1991, 14.

agents of God's reign and participate in the transforming struggle to realize freedom for all.[70]

For religious education to be purposeful, "knowing" and "being" must be united and, go beyond the source and nature of truth.[71] This extends beyond the "praxis way of knowing" in which we come to know truth through action and reflection together to enabling individuals to engage with the consciousness that arises from their entire 'being' as agent-subjects-in relationship.[72]

For Groome, *subject* means valuing people as people, in contrast to objects. However, the term "agent subject," highlights the active, reflective, responsible nature of human subjectivity without implying subordination. Agents-subjects-in relationship" captures the idea that authentic personhood does not arise in isolated self-sufficiency but through caring for and receiving care from others.[73]

This approach demonstrates a deeper grasp of the "learning outcome" of religious education, intended by the "shared praxis approach. The concept of "learning outcome" is no longer confined to what Western epistemology traditionally defines as "knowledge, but engages the entire person —mind, heart, and lifestyle—to inform, shape, and transform identity and agency within the world.[74]

---

[70] Ibid.17. Groome's treatment of the phrases 'reign of God,' 'lived Christian faith,' 'wholeness of human freedom that is fullness of life for all,' enriches our grasp of what is intended in this quotation.

[71] Ibid., 8.

[72] Groome, *Sharing,* 8.

[73] Ibid.

[74] Ibid., 7.

For this "learning outcome" to succeed, conation—biblical wisdom—must be attained[75] by overcoming "subjectivism and determinism," and fostering the innate drive for "authentic being" in all human beings, that motivates us to seek good and truth through action.[76] Connotative activity is a distinctly human characteristic that engages individuals' physical, cognitive, and volitional capacities—their intellect, emotions, and observable actions—as they cultivate an authentic sense of self within ethical relationships with others and the world, contributing in ways that are beneficial to all.[77]

When the 'learning outcome' is to be shaped by religious education, this implies that it must be 'being and becoming Christian' in the literal sense of the word. This involves educating people in Christian faith so they know, desire, and act with others according to Jesus' example and developing character that embodies belief, trust, and practice central to lived Christian faith.[78]

For Groome, wisdom can refer to a holistic human activity including cognition, affection, and volition that engages and shapes people's whole "being" in ways that are historically responsible and life-giving for self and others. It pertains to one's identity and agency and is realized in one's very "being." This wisdom comes from reflecting on life, learning from others, and understanding

---

[75] Ibid., 27. According to Groome, the ancient term 'conation' corresponds to the Hebrew Scriptures and the New Testament use of the term wisdom.

[76] Ibid., 29. Groome describes this drive as the passion to fulfil our human nature, constantly oriented toward the world and connected with others.

[77] Ibid., 30.

[78] Ibid.

God's teachings via Scripture and tradition. It grows within a community that tests and dialogues about it, aiming to shape people in faith, reflected through living out these values.[79]

The goal of the religious educational enterprise gives credence to the issues regarding the church's involvement in the world on behalf of the "reign of God." The implications of this perspective leave little doubt about what must be considered as the most constructive/productive approach to implementing a religious education program to achieve these learning outcomes.

Shared Christian Praxis

Freire points out three philosophical assumptions upon which his approach to education is grounded. First, humanization is the basic human vocation. That calling, however, is constantly prevented from being realized by dehumanizing cultural and social oppression. But while both humanization and dehumanization are alternatives, only the first is man's vocation. Second, people can change their reality to become creators of our culture, not merely determined by it. We can have a critical consciousness of our reality and act to change it. Third, education is never neutral, but has political consequences that can either control people by integrating them into conformity with existing society or liberate them to critically and creatively transform their reality.[80] He argued for this approach as

---

[79] Ibid., 32.
[80] Thomas H. Groome, *Religious education*, 175-176.

promoting human emancipation,"[81] the articulated purpose of religious education.[82]

Freire's endorses the concept of "critical consciousness" or conscientization that arises from reflection on their historical experience and disposes people to act. This process decodes and strips reality to uncover the myths that deceive and perpetuate the dominating structure. Then we can "change these structures by participating in historical, critical praxis."[83] The concept of the "praxis way of knowing" promotes "knowing" in the biblical sense, maintaining unity between "theory" and practice. It promotes a lived faith, that and reduces the gap between what we proclaim and the way we live. Further, it can promote emancipation and human freedom better than a "from theory to practice" concept.[84]

Components of Shared Christian Praxis

According to Groome, "religious education by shared praxis involves 'sharing critical reflection on present action in light of the Christian Story within Scripture and tradition and its vision of lived Christian faith." Since "present action is the consequence of our past and the shaper of our future," the group engages in reflection on "the historical self and society."[85] This activity helps us identify causes behind such action and understand its likely or intended

---

[81] Ibid, 175.
[82] See Groome, *Sharing*, 9, 29 and 32.
[83] Groome, *Religious education,* 176.
[84] Ibid., 177.
[85] Ibid., 184-185.

consequence.[86]

The effectiveness of this process is dependent on three forms of critical reflection: "critical reason," "critical memory," and "creative imagination." Critical reason evaluates the present "or attempts to notice the obvious, to apprehend rather than passively accept it as the way things are."[87] This "critical evaluative analysis" makes it possible "to discover the interest in present action, critique the ideology that maintains it, and recognize the assumptions on which it is based. It requires returning to the genesis of present action, and so we come to the role of memory.[88]

Critical memory seeks to "uncover the past in the present,"[89] "to get at the source of thinking"[90] so we can discover the personal and social genesis of our present action. In reflecting upon the source of our activity, we come to know our own story and to name our own constitutive knowing which arises from our engagement in the world. Without this element, our stories are forgotten, and the world is named for us.

Yet, critical reflection is incomplete if it rests only on reason and memory. Naming our present and knowing our story frees us to imagine and choose our future. Creative imagination allows us to presently envision the future"[91] as a "shaping activity that gives intentionality to the future as

---

[86] Ibid.
[87] Ibid., 195.
[88] Ibid., 185
[89] Ibid.
[90] Ibid., 186.
[91] Ibid.

it arises out of the past."[92] If properly engaged, it reshapes the present so that a "preferred" future will emerge.[93]

However, none works alone. While their functions differ, they cannot be separated. To bear fruit, "reason," "memory" and "imagination," must work together in critical reflection in the shared praxis approach because each serves a purpose. Memory connects us to the past; reason grounds us in the present, and imagination guides us toward the future. Memory is shaped by reason and imagination; reason relies on memory and imagination to interpret the present, and imagination draws from memory and is critiqued by reason.[94]

Notably, there is an affective dimension to this process with profound implications for human "being."[95] This is not a "debilitative negativism" but rather "an affirmation that recognizes what is good and true in present action, acknowledges its limitations, and attempts to move beyond them." Its success is not found in human capability but in the "Spirit's grace of discernment working within human effort" leading to knowing reality in light of God's activity and contributing to its transformation according to God's will."[96]

Dialogue is the most essential element in the shared praxis approach and the most effective way to form Christian community within the pedagogical setting.[97] If a

---

[92] Ibid.
[93] Ibid., 187.
[94] Ibid.
[95] Ibid.
[96] Ibid 188.
[97] Ibid.

group engages in Martin Buber's I/You relationship dialogue model, it will be formed into a true community. What is intended by dialogue in the shared praxis approach is not mere discussion, but "... the encounter in which the dialoguers' united reflection and action are addressed to the world that is to be transformed and humanized. Such dialogue cannot be reduced to one person depositing ideas in another, nor can it be a simple exchange of ideas to be 'consumed' by the discussants. It is neither a hostile, polemical argument between committed individuals nor the naming of the world.

Rather, the entire content and process of a shared praxis approach is dialogical and begins with oneself.[98] For as we dialogue with ourselves by truly listening to what is expressed by others and allowing them to disclose themselves.[99] True Christian community is formed in a context of love, trust and hope.[100]

In shared Christian praxis, the dialogue is not only among the participants but also between the participants and God. Very often, while listening to a participant tell his or her story, inner dialogue merges into dialogue with God. Sometimes praxis shared prayer is the most fitting response to what was being heard.[101]

The story is another component of shared Christian praxis. For "story" is "the whole faith tradition of a people however that is expressed or embodied." Specific roles and expected lifestyles, written scriptures, interpretations,

---

[98] Ibid.
[99] Ibid., 189.
[100] Ibid., 191.
[101] Ibid.

pious practices, sacraments, symbols, rituals, feast days, communal structures, artifacts, 'holy' places have emerged from this covenanted relationship. These embody, express, or re-create some part of the history of that covenant. The term is a metaphor for all such expressions of our faith tradition as part of our Christian Story. From that story, by God's grace, we draw our life of Christian faith, and by making it accessible again we experience God's saving deeds on our behalf.[102] With the Holy Spirit's help, using story as a benchmark for our reasoning and imagination enables us to discern God's will at a given moment.[103]

Dialectical Hermeneutics

The dialectical dimension involves three different, but not separated, movements: affirming, refusing, and moving beyond. Further, within a dialectical hermeneutic framework engaging with a "text" entail discerning the truths it affirms as well as recognizing the limitations inherent in our comprehension. This involves advancing beyond those constraints by integrating both the affirmed truths and newly acquired insights into ongoing understanding.[104]

This is a "positive and creative " activity in the shared Christian praxis approach since the "first affirming moment in the relationship... (being) is a positive one, and

---

[102] Ibid., 192.
[103] Ibid., 193.
[104] Ibid.,196

the third moment of moving beyond (becoming) is a creative and radical yes, rather than a debilitating no."[105]

This shared Christian praxis approach represents the most effective option for enabling the church to move beyond its limited perspective of its role as 'agent-subjects-in-relationship.' Otherwise, its mission of bearing witness to the 'reign of God,' is hindered by insufficient comprehension of the practical and social implications inherent in its calling.[106]

These activities are designed to ensure that the community's decisions aligned with the life-giving, vision of the reign of God. Groome offers three guidelines for accomplishing the end and preparing the ground for its final completion. So the proposed response must promote freedom, peace, justice, and wholeness.

Decisions must be made in continuity with the story of the Christian community before them. They cannot contradict what is essential to the story as discerned by the whole community/church from the earliest days of the Church to the present. For the Church as Christian community has always had the right to teach. Yet, no small community of Christians can be a reliable guide of truth in isolation from the rest of the Christian community. To claim as much would contradict the catholicity of Christianity.[107]

---

[105] Ibid.
[106] Ibid., 197.
[107] Ibid., 199.

Implementing the Shared Praxis Approach

Groome uses five movements to describe how the shared praxis approach should work. While there is nothing sacrosanct about the "number five" and other educators may adjust, combine, or increase the movements, a consideration of these movements is now in order.

First movement: Naming Present Action

The educator presents a topic for discussion and reflection with the goal of having each participant name their present action in response to the focus of the unit." This may be any action intentionally or deliberately, of one's own 'knowing' (doing) as it arises from engagement with the world.[108]

Second Movement: The Participants' Stories and Visions

The educator promotes "critical reflection," encouraging all participants to examine their motivations and goals in relation to the topic. This increases awareness of social norms and assumptions influencing their actions. This can be achieved using critical memory to probe biography and trying to uncover the social influences on our story. It entails the use of imagination as we attempt to ascertain the likely consequences of our action and release dialogue that was previously repressed.[109]

---

[108] Ibid., 209.
[109] Ibid.,211.

Third Movement: Christian Community's Story and Vision

Here, attention is given to how the Christian community's story shapes perspectives or attention and response within the context of the reign of God.[110] This involves the traditioning process or "handing down, of what has come to us over our past pilgrimage." The story must, be framed "in a dialogical manner, as personal understanding that can give life, rather than as barren dogmatism that arrests the journey toward maturity and faith."[111]

The story/vision must be disclosed in a way that invites people to reflect upon, grapple with, and question their stories and visions, as they encounter what is being presented. Thus, the presenter must never make his or her version of the community story/vision the final statement of the 'truth or other participants are unlikely to dialogue with their own lived experience.

Fourth Movement: Dialectical Hermeneutic Between Story and Participants' Stories

The educator helps facilitate a "critique of the story in light of the stories and a critique of the participants' present stories in light of the past story."[112] The dialectical activity comes into play in asking what the community's story means for our stories. We seek to see if it affirms, calls in question, or invites beyond our story, and if our stories

---

[110] Ibid., 214.

[111] Ibid., 215.

[112] Ibid.

(affirm, recognize limits of, push beyond the community's story).[113]

Since our understanding of the story is limited, we can never exhaust its meaning and truth for our lives. The ground of our story is a God of ultimate mystery and thus no version or understanding we have of God's activity can ever be the last word. Rather than passively accepting, or simply repeating, the accessible version, we must recognize and attempt to move beyond our present understanding. The educator must ensure that he lived faith experience must be informed by the Christian faith tradition, and appropriation of the tradition must be informed by, and in the context of, lived faith experience."[114]

Fifth Movement: Dialectical Hermeneutic Between the Vision and Participants' Visions.

Participants' visions are assessed in relation to the larger "reign of God" vision. For we want to understand whether our current actions support the vision, and how we should act in the future. Thus, individuals can select a faith response— a Christian praxis— based on all that has gone before." This activity enables us to see signs of the reign of God already among us, while perceiving and responding to its not-yetness in our lives. [115]

This movement is essential if our religious education is to lead to further Christian praxis," because "Christian faith is a whole way of being in the world, a lived response rather

---

[113] Ibid.
[114] Ibid., 220.
[115] Ibid.

than a theory about it, and our religious education should invite people to decision." This must be "an opportunity for choosing built in as a consistent part of the process, rather than simply taken for granted."

While this is no simple task, the Shared Praxis approach should be central to any program that attempts to enable churches to address the issues of social justice because it lends itself to aiding us in engaging the world.

Finally, using this approach fosters an open environment where participants contribute to the learning experience and outcomes. For, no one has all the knowledge. While the story is the north star in the unfolding process, one's perception of it is not sacralized and is open to critique.

This method promotes dialogue instead of argument as participants are encouraged to reason about their faith and daily decisions. The polemics that characterize most interactions about church polity or doctrine can be minimized or eliminated. By realizing that there are other stories and visions, the potential for authentic spiritual growth and maturity can take place.

Implementing these practices at the grassroots level can positively influence church communities, moving members from simply knowing about God's reign to embodying it in their everyday lives. Ultimately, participants will be enabled to identify and address oppressive conditions, and embrace the freedom intended within God's community.

Conclusion

The problem with the African American Pentecostal church is not with its capability to respond since the financial, physical, and intellectual resources are adequate. The issue is indifference to issues of social, economic, and racial injustice. The question is how could a church not be moved to action against the dehumanizing forces rampant in the communities where tit has been established to bring hope and meaning?

Underlying this indifference and other-worldly preoccupation, is a theology that conditioned many Pentecostals to see their only duty to the world as preaching the Gospel and keeping themselves unspotted. The near obsession with the Rapture precludes many from engaging in social or political matters despite the Lord's command to be active in changing the world so that it may become more God glorifying.

Most African American Apostolics hold the understanding that after the church has secured the world for Christ, He will return to reign in His earthly kingdom. They see human history as an ongoing struggle between cosmic forces with the victory of righteousness assured. Since a postmillennialist position is anathema to them, they simply await in the *Parousia* and see no reason to be involved in transforming the world.

However, this sharp separation of the natural and supernatural was not the position of early Pentecostals. Rather, they addressed the totality of human existence.

The understanding that Christians should participate with God in confronting the evil forces at work in the world was part of the seventeenth and eighteenth-century Wesleyan revivals and the Holiness movement, though it mainly encompassed social welfare. But it did not continue in the first quarter of the twentieth century. At the turn of the twentieth century, however J. Nelson Darby's premillennialist dispensationalist theology influenced leaders such as Moody and was popularized by Scofield as the only right Scriptural interpretation among some Fundamentalists and independent Pentecostal groups.

Skillfully illustrated Scofieldian charts, graphs, and pictures that could be easily mastered provided a sense of authority and absoluteness. Independent Holiness and Pentecostal churches used his Bible, with emphasis on the secret escape, and its dispensational schema regarding the failure of humankind to change in the world, as their major teaching resource. This led them to believe there was nothing required of them, and they should not be involved with worldly problems since the Lord would take care of these things upon his return. Secular agencies were left to deal with society's problems and no prophetic word, no speaking of truth to power, came from the church.

Yet, Scripture provides alternative insights regarding the church's role in the world. In the Sermon on the Mount, Jesus' word his disciples, as well as the church challenges us to be in, but not of, the world in transformative ways.[116]

To respond in obedience to this command, the church must look at its implications through the theological-cultural lens of 'salt' and 'light, taking agency for effecting transformation. Transformative religious education can

---

[116] Matt. 5:13-16 and John 17:16

facilitate the liberation for which all people strive. Its neglect leads to the uncritical acceptance of the Scofieldian perspectives that have limited stewardship and are focused on indoctrination into this inadequate world view.

The Shared Christian Praxis approach to Christian education is the most compatible with the goal of working toward transforming society and dislodging the church from the constraints and stagnation of an inadequate teaching method. The emphasis on dialogue among the participants offers hope for a level of sharing regarding the Christian story and the church's life that can unmask the traditionalism that has muddied the waters and obscured the life-giving power of the Gospel.

Some may fear that important doctrinal teachings could be abandoned, and the church could become too worldly. Yet, the benefits to the church's witness justify this risk. Hopefully, educators/facilitators will embrace this approach, as a way of ministering to and with others to bring about the personal transformation essential to the church's becoming a transforming presence in the world at a new level of service to the reign of God.

Scofield's view positioned the church as second to Israel and primarily confined its relevant scriptural passages to the epistles. The Hebrew Scripture and Jesus' focus on the reign of God were construed as referring to Israel and the coming reign and only addressing the disciples and the Jewish nation until their rejection of His Messianic role. Accordingly, the church was regarded as a mystery awaiting its unveiling at Jesus' return. Its rewards were reserved for heaven and its mission limited to saving souls and ensuring the faithful perseverance of believers until death or the Lord's return.

85

Bibliography

Anderson, Robert Mapes. *Vision of the Disinherited: The Making of American Pentecostalism,* Oxford University Press, 1979.

Aulen, Gustaf *Jesus in Contemporary Historical Research*. Translated by Ingalill H. Hjelm. Philadelphia: Fortress Press, 1976.

Barr, James *Fundamentalism.* Philadelphia: Westminster Press,1978. 193-94.

Boys, Mary. *Educating in Faith: Maps and Visions.* Raleigh, NC: Academic Renewal Press, 2001.

Bruner, Emil. *Eternal Hope.*

Cartwright, Michael G. "Wrestling with Scripture: Can Euro-American Christians & African-American Christians Learn to Read Scripture Together?", Downers Grove, IL: Intervarsity Press, 197.

Charles C. Ryrie, Dispensationalism Today. Chicago: Moody Press, 1981.

Church of Our Lord Jesus Christ of the Apostolic Faith, Inc., "General Annual Convocation Minute Book and Ministerial Record of The Eightieth Session Held at Detroit, Michigan, August 13-19

Cremin, Lawrence A. *American Education: The Metropolitan Experience 1876-1980.* New York: Harper & Row, Publishers, 1988.

Daniels, David D. "The Cultural Renewal of Slave Religion: Charles Price Jones and the Emergence of the Holiness Movement in Mississippi, Ph.D. Dissertation, Union Theological Seminary, 1992

Dayton, Donald. *The Theological Roots of Pentecostalism. Waco, TX: Baker Academic, 1987.*

Discipline Book, The Church of Our Lord Jesus Christ of the Apostolic Faith, Inc. 6th edition, 1991. New York: Office of The Executive Secretary, 1961.

Douglas Frank, *Less Than Conquerors: How Evangelicals Entered the*

Twentieth Century. Grand Rapids, MI: Wm. B. Eerdmans
Publishers, 1996.

Freire, Paulo. *Pedagogy of the Oppressed*. Myra Bergman Ramos, Trans.
New York: Continuum, 1992.

Groome, Thomas H. *Sharing Faith: A Comprehensive Approach to
Religious Education & Pastoral Ministry. The Way of Shared Praxis*.
New York, New York: Harper Collins, 1991.

___________________., *Christian Religious Education: Sharing Our Story
and Vision*. New York: HarperCollins Publishers, 1980,

Lawson, Robert C. "The Ministry of Women in the Church" *The
Contender for the Faith*, April 1958,.

Leech, Kenneth "Spirituality and Social Justice" in Chelsy Jones,
Geoffrey Wainwright and Edward Yarnold, eds., *The Study of
Spirituality*. New York: Oxford University Press, 1986.

Lincoln, C. Eric and Lawrence Mamiya, *The Black Church in the
African America Experie*nce. Durham: Duke University Press, 1990.

Lovett, Leonard "Black Holiness-Pentecostalism: Implications for
Ethics and Social Transformation." Ph.D. diss. Emory University,
Atlanta, GA, 1978.

Marsden, George *Fundamentalism and American Culture: The Shaping of
the Twentieth-Century Evangelicalism 1870-1925*. New York: Oxford
University Press, 1980.

Marty, Martin E. *Modem American Religion*. Vol. 1. Chicago, Ill.: The
University of Chicago Press, 1986.

Niebuhr, H. Richard *Christ and Culture*. New York: Harper Torch
Books, 1951.

Pazmino, Robert W. Pazmino, *Principles & Practices of Christian
Education: An Evangelical Perspective*. Grand Rapids, MI: Baker Book
House, 1992,

Prosser, Peter E. *Dispensationalist Eschatology and Its Influence on
American and British Religious Movements*. Lewiston: Edwin Mellen
Press, 1999.

Reed, David Arthur. "Origin and Development of the Theology of Oneness Pentecostalism in the United States," Ph.D. diss. Boston University Graduate School, Boston, MA, 1978.

Scofield, C. I. *Scofield Reference Bible*, New York: Oxford University Press, 1998.

Scott-King, Coretta and Martin Luther King, Jr. *The Words of Martin Luther King, Jr.* New York: William Morrow Paperbacks, 2001.

Synan, Vinson. *The Holiness Pentecostal Movement.* Grand Rapids: Wm. B. Eerdmans, 1971.

Torrey, Rueben A., A.C. Dixon, et al, editors, *The Fundamentals - A Testimony to the Truth.* 12 vols. Chicago: Testimony Publishing Co., 1910–1915.

Tyson, J. Laverne. *Before I Sleep: A Narrative and Photographic Biography of Bishop Garfield Thomas Haywood*, Weldon Spring, MO: Pentecostal Publishing House, 1976.

Wilmore, Gayraud "Black Religious Traditions," in William R. Scott & William G. Shade, editors, *Upon These Shores: Themes in the African-American Experience, 1600 to the Present.* New York: Routledge, 2000

Index

World, 2, 12, 15-17, 18, 36
Postmillennialism, 21, 22, 23
Premillennialism, 2, 5, 20, 22,
    23, 25, 26, 28, 31, 32, 36, 44
Prosser, Peter, 8n., 20n., 23n.,
    28n., 39

Rapture, the, 25, 28, 44, 47, 80

Scofield,
Scofield Reference Bible, 26,
    30n., 33, 35
Seymour, William Joseph, 7-
    10, 11
Synan, Vinson, 8n., 9n., 10n.

Torrey, Rueben A., 4, 24, 32

Wilmore, Gayraud, 18, 36

9 781967 034291